Globalization and Human Resource Management in the Airline Industry

Second edition

JACK EATON

Ashgate

Aldershot • Burlington USA • Singapore • Sydney

Published by
Ashgate Publishing Ltd
Gower House
Croft Road
Aldershot
Hants GU11 3HR
England

Ashgate Publishing Company
131 Main Street
Burlington, VT 05401-5600 USA

Ashgate website: http://www.ashgate.com

British Library Cataloguing in Publication Data
Eaton, Jack
    Globalization and human resource management in the airline
    industry. - 2nd ed. - (Ashgate studies in aviation
    economics and management)
    1.Airlines - Personnel management
    I.Title
    387.7'0683

Library of Congress Control Number: 00-110603

ISBN 0 7546 1286 4

Printed and bound in Great Britain by MPG Books Ltd, Bodmin, Cornwall

Contents

Preface

Since the first edition of this book in 1996, there might be cause to question the title. Globalization was then prominent in the strategic plans of major airlines. BA had announced a strategy of globalization in the early 1990s and accordingly, had embarked on a series of mergers in Europe, Australia and the USA. The megacarriers of the USA, American and United, so alarmed Bernard Attali, then president of Air France, that he espoused a defensive strategy of consolidation and rationalization. Previously state-owned airlines were privatized and put into the globalization contest.

In this contest, the European and US carriers apparently faced fierce competition from the Asia-Pacific region. Their costs were relatively high and the principal element accounting for the difference was human resource management. Whatever the rights and wrongs of deregulation, it has had a huge effect, especially in confirming a global labour market in aviation. Intensified competition has squeezed yields, despite improved yield management techniques associated with computerized reservation systems. Scrutiny of human resource management is inevitable because raising productivity and cutting costs are among the limited areas in the industry where management retains some control. Simply by analogy with 'flagging out' in ocean transport, there are potentially drastic effects on labour costs.

Even to move slightly in this direction by attempted globalizing strategies has exacerbated the tension between maintaining staff morale – essential in a business that depends on customer service – and raising productivity or reducing labour costs. Both the latter tend to mean deteriorating working conditions. Problems in recalculating this equation, the effort bargain, have thwarted the challenge of several Asian carriers whose managements could not contain costs and prevent overt conflict, including JAL and Cathay Pacific. By comparison, SIA has developed a learning organization that seems to come close to the 'control by commitment' that is the ideal of human resource management.

Cost-cutting and the consequent human resource management effects have figured in the strategies of BA and the big US companies. For BA, the human factor was decisive in its fall from blue chip to stock market lame duck and Robert Ayling's leadership was called to account. The transformational leadership often associated with strategic human resource management and aimed at changed corporate culture and quantum leaps in organizational performance does not seem to work in large airlines. Robert Crandall's style at American also incited conflict, while Gerald Greenwald struggled to prevent friction between flight attendants and management at United, despite the improving profitability of the airline. The transformational approach seemed appropriate only in smaller, short haul airlines, such as Southwest under Herb Kelleher and Ryanair where Michael O'Leary successfully applied the same no frills formula.

Globalization has also been held to be a myth, largely because it runs against the international arrangements for landing rights by means of bilateral treaties between countries. The continuing failure of the UK and USA governments to renegotiate their treaty (together with competition requirements from the European Union) effectively scuppered the planned alliance of BA and American and may be instrumental in obstructing BA's planned merger with KLM. Yet, although the process is slower than expected, the global trends continue. Technologically, they mainly occur through computerized reservation systems and direct online reservations. Here the CRS companies acted as learning organizations but that learning was also externalized as major airlines' operations managers learned how to do without travel agents and began to squeeze them. Organizationally, they develop as airlines operations and marketing managers form strategic alliances to try to calm competition by collusion and saving transactions costs.

The structure of the book has been left basically unchanged. Within this framework, however, many of the empirical examples have been revised or replaced. Again the book does not aspire to be comprehensive. The theme remains that globalization has been noted as a feature of recent industrial and commercial developments and that the airline business might be expected to be at the forefront – with concomitant effects on human resource management.

Human resource management has passed into management and journalistic parlance, but it remains a controversial phrase. The author's attitude to it is the reason for the arrangement of the book into four parts. Parts I and II are about the organization of airlines as businesses. Part I indicates that the primary impetus for human resource management springs from the perceived need among airline managers for their businesses to be market-driven, rather than operations-driven. Part II is a more theoretical view of the internal organizational implications, concentrating on sub-contracting.

Part III is just one chapter, but in many ways it is a pivotal chapter for the book because it is an analysis of the constitutional change in the industrial relations – or rules governing the management of employment in the industry. The main comparative examples used as BA and Air France and how their managements handled the conflictful industrial relations issues arising from attempted changes in the deployment of human resources after 1996.

Paradoxically, although it is associated with market-led management, human resource management is also extolled as a strategic, integrative approach. The extent of this integration with production management, financial management and the continuing need for a norm-setting function in the management of personnel are discussed in Part IV, Human Resource Management and other management functions.

Airline managers are even more secretive and defensive about academic research than those in other industries. The author is obliged to those few who did provide assistance but also to the several employees, who, justifiably cautious, gave helpful information. Thanks are due to the International Association of Women Airline Pilots (ISA) for granting permission to quote from the survey on harassment and discrimination and publisher McGraw-Hill for permission to use extracts from 'Management Rights and Union Interests'. Among colleagues who, despite being under the pressure to publish for research assessment, nevertheless, generously supplied useful references, I would like to thank Jenny Poolton. The copy was efficiently typed and prepared by Linda Jones.

Dr. Jack Eaton,
Aberystwyth, 2000

PART I
EXTERNAL RELATIONS

1 Relations with Customers

In 1987, shortly after privatization BA management proclaimed that it was now a 'customer first' company. Even amidst the welter of hype and public relations that characterized the last years of the twentieth century, this was remarkable. Hasn't the commercial maxim always been that the customer is always right? Why was there any need to state it and what relationship does it have with human resource management?

The rationale was the management doctrine known as Total Quality Management (TQM). Here, 'quality' does not refer to excellence but to 'fitness for use', such that the product or service is fit to keep the customer satisfied or, better still, that the customer is 'constantly delighted'. The service that airlines produce is 'arrivals' or happy landings. The 'total' in Total Quality Management refers to the objective of injecting customer relations into all stages of the production process in order to ensure that all staff are responsible for quality and contribute to satisfied customers. This is far from straightforward when we think of one customer among the millions of those transported by the big airline carriers.

Oakland (1993) quoted an apposite example. A flight attendant has a trolley full of breakfasts to feed the early morning business passengers on the short domestic flight into an international airport. The first tray is returned with a complaint that bread roll and jam are missing. The attendant's composure disintegrates on discovering more trays with the roll and jam missing, necessitating a search for complete trays. This is clearly a problem of quality - but not at the attendant's work yet rather, in the organization with a person whose job it is to assemble the breakfast trays. (It might not even be *in* the organization but with a catering contractor.)

Total Quality Management is an approach to improving the effectiveness and flexibility of business as a whole. Essentially, it is a way of organizing and involving the whole organization; every department, every activity, every single person at every level. For an organization to be fully effective, each part of it must work together, recognizing interdependence. TQM, according to Oakland, is a method for ridding people's lives of wasted effort by involving everyone in the process of improvement; improving the effectiveness of work so that results can be achieved in less time. TQM is primarily to ensure that the management adopts a strategic view of quality - developing the 'prevention is better than cure' mentality. Add to that empowerment of employees, in the sense of involvement in teamworking, and it could be quite a fruitful technique in the context of the 'learning organization'.

Implications for Human Resource Management in Airlines

However, many people are in favour of goodness and against evil. Who will admit to being in favour of poor quality? What is important about TQM is how to implement it. Managements that rely on exhortation of the workforce to 'do this job right first time' or 'accept that quality is *your* responsibility' will not only fail to achieve quality but will create division and conflict. Involvement of all members is needed for company-wide quality improvement.

It is pertinent to begin a study of human resource management with relations with customers and with TQM because the injection of market relations into all points in the production process is one of the aspirations of human resource management - as opposed to administrative-style personnel management. If TQM is a strategy for performance management and human resource management purports to be strategic personnel management, then they are in tandem. All management is to some extent about control of employees. Human resource management has been characterized as entailing a move from control of employees by means of rules (the 'Industrial Relations' model) to control by gaining the commitment of employees.

Total Quality Management by means of empowering employees with responsibility for quality of production is one route to achieving this but it is far from unproblematic and, actually, raises tensions and contradictions that are possibly inevitable. After all, why should subordinate employees be responsible for quality when they are not the primary stakeholders of a company? It may be a matter of corporate survival and thereby saving jobs but this is somewhat different from empowerment. Potentially, empowerment may be compatible with the Japanese model of the firm as a collection of human resources (Odagiri, 1984). Making market demand immanent by introduction of internal markets, of chains of suppliers and internal customers is much less benevolent with the shareholder control model of the firm. For example, a study by Fuller and Smith (1991) showed systematic use of customer feed back mechanisms, including the employment of impostor customers, to control the behaviour of employees in contact with customers. It might be thought that this is fair enough but it also has shades of coercion. The American originators of TQM insisted that 85 per cent of faults are management's responsibility. 'Empowering' employees with this responsibility begins to sound rather like totalitarian quality management.

Relations with Customers in Practice - the Role of TQM

That everyone in the production process must try to satisfy customer needs that are not only external but also those of the next people in the production process is the hall-mark of TQM. Concomitantly, it is the customer relations aspect of human resource management. How and when did it appear in air transport and how does it operate in practice? Raising such questions may provide a basis for assessing whether TQM in airlines is a way of giving employees more responsible autonomy and control over their working lives or whether it is just another, more or less sophisticated, way for senior management to gain more direct control over the subordinate employees. This is a key issue in human resource management and therefore a key theme of this book. It is true that Total Quality Management has, like many other management techniques before it, gone somewhat out of fashion but its influence on the origins of human resource management remains seminal.

The End of the Golden Age

By the late 1970s it was arguable that the glamour and glory had departed from most air travel. To some extent, it is a positional good in that it comprises social relations 'subject to congestion or crowding through more extensive use'. (Hirsch, 1977:27). Everyone spoils it a bit for everyone else. Sometime during the 1970s it became clear that there was over-capacity in the airline industry. The airlines, with market share and profits under threat, inaugurated strategies to achieve more 'cost-efficient' flying. Deregulation, begun under the Carter administration in the USA and continued under the Reagan administration, exacerbated the tendency. The airlines began using planes that could hold more people and fly longer hours without fuel stops. For flight crews this led to 'longer work days and more work days bunched together. There was less time to relax and enjoy a central advantage of the work - personal travel. Like the aeroplane, the flight attendant was now kept in use as long as possible'. (Hochschild, 1989: 121).

With the deregulation of the airlines, the prices of tickets dropped and 'discount' customers boarded in even larger numbers. Consequently, in the 1980s, faced with increasing competition, airline managements attempted to intensify work through lay offs and job cuts in order to have more done by fewer. 'Before the speed-up, workers sustained the cheerful goodwill that good service requires. They did so far the most part proudly; they supported the transmutation. After the speed-up, when asked to make a personal human contact at inhuman speed, they cut back on emotional work and grew detached.' (Hochschild : 121). On this view, TQM was necessary to reinforce customer care. Also a more cheap and cheerful version of TQM was much more readily introduced by the gadfly short-haul carriers that had begun to encroach on the majors' markets.

Relations with Customers, Prices and TQM   *Total quality management*

After the Airline Regulation Act 1978, many new U.S. airlines were certified. There was a rapid increase in the number of carriers and fierce competition with the new entrants in particular seeking to expand market share. There were fare wars and the U.S. industry operated at a loss between 1979 and 1987, a picture repeated for the industry globally during the post Gulf War recession and over-capacity of the 1990s. The fare wars stimulated air travel but forced all airlines to cut operating costs.

People Express was founded in 1981. There was no corporate hierarchy and no rigid job specialisation. Everyone was an owner-manager because every employee was required to buy 100 shares in the company. A pilot was a 'flight manager' and a flight attendant a 'customer-service manager'. Everyone was 'cross-utilised'. The flight manager might do inventory control and the customer-service manager might work at the ticket counter. The company also did away with the traditional standard services, such as free meals, free baggage handling and comfortable lounges. Consequently, the high employee motivation, low labour costs and elimination of 'frills' made it possible for People Express to offer very cheap fares that made flight travel more popular, (Chen and Meindl, 1991 : 529).

At first it was successful but its ultimate failure begins to point up the dilemmas that TQM attempts to answer. There were increasing passenger complaints about delayed flights, lost luggage and overbooking. The leadership became authoritarian and increasingly unable to tolerate dissent. As People Express encountered a more turbulent environment, its flatter hierarchy and its innovative human resources strategy began to dissipate, apart from the poor service and delays to customers. Employees were not allowed to question decisions any more and fear pervaded the company. People Express became known as 'People Distress'. Finally it was sold to Texas Air. Yet the trick of 'cheap and cheerful' can be pulled off as it was by Southwest in the USA and Ryanair in Europe.

Fare wars and discounting were internationalized in the recession of the 1990s. It created a problem for corporate management of how and when to restore prices and profit margins. Price wars are high profile affairs as the combatants have to tell potential customers that they are cutting prices. In summer 1992 when U.S. domestic airlines were scrapping for customers, they started offering a return fare New York - Los Angeles for just $199. Tens of thousands of travellers came to have the money illusion that $199 was the 'right' price and anything else must be a rip-off. For the traveller, this situation was a joy, for the airlines a nightmare. So another function of the emphasis on quality is to provide a rationale to restore prices and margins by creating the illusion of service.

Southwest did manage to make money by offering a viable no-frills service on the People Express model and has been profitable for 24 consecutive years. It became the seventh largest carrier in the USA by flying short routes, offering no meals, just peanuts and drinks, doing without a first class and not assigning seats. Gate agents issued reusable numbered plastic cards on a first-come, first-served basis. The crucial factor, however, was successful implementation of human resource management on the commitment model. Its success was much influenced by the leadership of Herb Kelleher; rather than talking about himself, he preferred highlight the types of employees Southwest tries to attract and how they act on their own to help customers.

By contrast, the biggest carriers have to maintain international infrastructure, and fleets that preclude such an approach. Their only strategy is more intensive use of plant and planes. Compared to industry averages, Southwest had fewer employees per aircraft (79 against 131) and flew more passengers per employee. It also had low staff turnover and highly motivated employees. The 'hands-on' approach of chief executive, Herb Kelleher, no doubt contributed. Yet such a strategy has its limits - when competitors fight back and the environment becomes more turbulent, diminishing returns set in.

One technology that has helped in this respect is use of computerized reservation systems (CRS). The CRS has dramatically altered the relationship between airlines and their customers. As will be explained more fully later, CRS, though generally perceived as a marketing tool, are more properly a means of production management in airlines. In the competitive environment, such yield-management systems enable data on passenger demand for each flight to be gathered and analysed and optimal fares to be extrapolated. Airlines using such techniques gain a competitive advantage. Management acquires real-time data on changing market trends, enabling it immediately to adopt capacity, schedules and prices in response to such trends. Here human resource management is seen in its *resource* aspect.

Human resource management in this sense tends towards human asset accounting - with employees open to being fully utilised throughout working hours, rather than sometimes being able to find breathing spaces or slack time as a result of half-filled planes or unexpected pauses in demand. Employees, as Gerald Mars (1982 : 182), put it, 'attempt to stay loose in a tightening world'. It is increasingly difficult for them to do so. 'Because work is more easily monitored and measured, the porosity between work and non-work diminishes.' (Winfield, 1991 : 86) and 'one is increasingly paid only for what one does'. (Winfield : 104).

The 'human' aspect of human resource management with respect to TQM necessitates more fully insinuating responsibility for customer service onto each employee. This is much more difficult to achieve, the main approach being to 'empower' the employee, so to speak, with such responsibility. If this is accepted, then workers will monitor each other's performance. Although this sounds manipulative and can be just that, it does have some positive features. For one thing, on it may hinge sheer survival of part or all of the organization and consequently, employees' jobs. Two case study examples that follow illustrate this.

For the first, the author is indebted to Heather Hopfle's case study (1993) of British Airways. At the start of the 1980s BA had been a joke. Drastic job cuts then brought costs under control but customer service was seen as critical. Sir Colin Marshall, appointed chief executive in 1983, saw the need 'to create some motivational vehicle with the employees to raise their morale and, in turn, customer service.' (Young, 1989 : 3). He reckoned that staff would have to learn how to sell the airline and its services which led to the campaign known as 'Putting the Customer First'. This, in turn, led to a massive training programme called 'Putting People First' that aimed to provide an 'emotional context' for people to respond to and to change. Staff became actively involved in developing ideas for customer service. Customer First teams, using quality circle techniques, were formed in many BA departments. Quite suddenly, administrative procedures, formerly the task of personnel management, were devolved to line management, one of the features of human resource management.

The approach - a fashionable one at the time - was to present organizational change as necessitating a change in corporate culture. However, as Hopfle concluded, the reaction to the change was not all positive. Some staff found it difficult to reconcile the values promoted by the culture change with their own experiences in the workplace. There was some frustration and disillusionment as a result of the conflicts between caring values and profits and between espoused values and the need for workplace expediency. Some felt that their emotions were being played on in a rather manipulative way. More recently, with the decline in enthusiasm for TQM, out-and-out emotional management is seen as desirable and not something to be hidden.

The second example is discussed more fully in the final chapter. In 1989 KLM Cargo based at Heathrow was in serious financial difficulty and the main KLM board at Schipol was contemplating its closure. Local management copied the teamworking concept from the Nissan plant in Sunderland. The results were remarkable in terms of productivity and employee involvement.

Teamworking is a ubiquitous feature of TQM. However, the potential incompatibility between teamworking and the individualistic practices often associated with human resource management, such as performance appraisal and performance related pay, is often skated over. One management consultant almost revered by the Japanese who did not evade this tension was W. Edwards Deming. Actually, Deming did not even use the term 'Total Quality Management'. He believed that such a label made his thinking into a system, 'whereas he tended to perceive his thinking more as a philosophy and wished to have it seen that way'. (White & Wolf, 1995:204) However, he did emphasise statistical process control as part of his approach to quality improvement. The hallmark of this approach is that it requires management to compile accurate descriptive data about how a work process is functioning. Records must be kept of how many errors a workteam is making in performing a job. Among the techniques used are flow charts, Pareto charts and cause-effect or fishbone charts.

Change is directed at the work system itself, as in Deming's view, 'only a small percentage of the problems that an organization has in its processes is traceable to the worker. Hence the optimal strategy for improving performance is to direct attention for change at the system itself.' (White & Wolf:212). Deming's TQM started from the statistical principle that variation must be accepted as a reality and that most variation stems from general causes that exist in the organizational system itself, rather than the worker. Also, Deming has been heard to say that when a TQM culture is in place and people are working in teams and are rewarded as teams, the culture will drive out the few problem people who might be there.

An idea in this tradition emanated from the airline industry itself. It is called 'Moments of Truth' and was propounded by Jan Carlzon, chief executive of Scandinavian Airlines. They are the moments when a customer first comes into contact with the people, systems, procedures or products of an organization and which consequently influence the judgement that the customer makes about the quality of that organisation's services or products.

According to Oakland (1993: 233-34), in Moments of Truth analysis, 'the points of potential dissatisfaction are identified proactively, beginning with the assembly of process flow chart diagrams. Every small step taken by a customer in his/her dealings with the organization's people, products or services is recorded. It may be difficult or impossible to identify all the Moments of Truth but the systematic approach should lead to the minimization of the number and severity of the expected failures.'

Criticism of TQM

An important aspect of this book is the link that Carlzon purports to make between organisational strategy and tactics. In practice, the gimmicky title, 'Moments of Truth', and its popular usage with emphasis on the first 15 second encounter between a passenger and front-line staff may lead to people to ignore the importance of this link. Questioned about the type of strategy pursued by Delta Airlines, Stephan Egli, the vice-president for Europe, replied that one of the objectives is to offer a better product each day. (Gonzalez, 2000).

In recent years, one organization after another has announced the establishment of customer care programmes and many management consultants have joined the bandwagon. In many cases the results have been less than satisfactory - often because one or both of the following mistakes have been made.

First, only front-line contact staff have been the recipients of training. Carlzon makes it clear that if this occurs, the best efforts of front-line staff to satisfy customers may be blocked by back-room staff, the reason for this being that people in such positions, because of the measures used to assess their competence as well as their training and business experience, are seldom customer-oriented (let alone market-oriented). The result is, of course, demoralized contact staff and the possibility of the organization entering a vicious circle. (Blois, 1992 : 6)

Secondly, the link between tactics and strategy has not actually been made. Consequently, contact staff know little more than that they should be 'nice' to customers. However, the failure to have a clear and well-implemented strategy leaves such staff either with no understanding of how to operationalise that 'niceness' or, even if understanding how to behave, unable to act because of their organization's bureaucratic systems.

The BA and KLM episodes reported above are apparently positive examples of TQM application. However, before being carried away by its benefits, it is necessary to remind ourselves of its corporate rationale to create an aura of 'service' in a production process that became intensified as demand expanded in the 1980s and then as airline competition intensified with deregulation and recession. Hochschild, in her percipient study of the management of the emotional labour necessitated by in-flight service, tellingly quotes the editors of an unofficial flight attendants' newsletter, the 'Pan Am Quipper':

'We deal in the illusion of good service. We want to make passengers think they are having a good time. It is dangerous to take any of the abuse seriously. It is dangerous to take the job too seriously. Quipper is about laughing it off.'

This is not just bloody-mindednesses or flippancy. The author of this book has direct experience of how an airline company's objective to maximize plane capacity by filling every available seat and maximizing seating in the available space can potentially conflict with TQM - despite one of the objectives of TQM being to compensate for possible over-crowding. On a flight from London to Amsterdam, flight attendants were distributing lunch containers and serving drinks - a task that, together with clearing up - would occupy most of the 50-55 minutes flying time. There was a blind passenger seated in the row behind me. In attempting to attend to the requests of the blind person's travelling companion that he wanted a drink but not a meal, a flight attendant accidentally upset a jug of scalding hot coffee over a passenger in the centre aisle. Although reacting quickly by pouring cold water over the injured passenger, the damage was done and, apart from personal attention to his scalds during the rest of the flight, would doubtless necessitate recompense later. It was certainly not a quality flight for him.

How this 'moment of truth' resulted for the flight attendant concerned is not known. However, the moment of truth was evidently acted upon, as on the return flight there was no attempt to distribute drinks, a lunch container and then coffee. Travellers in tourist class were offered only a choice of sandwich and a drink, soft or alcoholic, but cold.

TQM in airlines is also contradicted by the findings of the US Consumers' Union that airlines are saving millions by switching off ventilation systems to the discomfort of unsuspecting passengers. A report in the UK Consumer Association's 'Holiday Which?' magazine summarized the American research, claiming that 747 crews can choose to operate systems normally or reduce the flow of fresh and circulated air - saving fuel and money. The American Association of Flight Attendants noted that little research has been done on the effect of poor air quality. However, 'recent international research seems to indicate that cabin crew are occupationally exposed to a range of health and safety risks, about which they receive little - if any – information'. (Boyd & Bain, 1998:17) The rapid scattering of crew and passengers makes it difficult to detect a clump of illness from spread infection of effects similar to those of 'sick building syndrome' via diseases such as colds, flu, measles and tuberculosis.

Finally, TQM loses all credibility in the face of marketing gimmicks, such as that operated by Japan Airlines. In 1994 JAL was demanding that its female flight attendants dress up as Minnie Mouse, with mouse ears, headbands with red polka dot bows and aprons decorated with Disney characters. JAL's ostensible reason for the gimmick was to regain passengers and revenue after three successive years of losses. However, some of the flight attendants suspected an ulterior motive - a twisted link between organizational tactics and strategy. They were being forced to look ridiculous so that they would quit their jobs, helping JAL in its aim to cut staff from 22,000 to 17,000. JAL spent 350 million yen on license fees to Disney and to paint three aircraft with Disney characters. Not only were the cabin crew expected to wear the Minnie Mouse costume but also to sell Disney goods. Male flight attendants were not expected to dress up as Mickey Mouse as that costume would clash with the formal evening wear that they must wear in-flight. There is clearly a great contradiction with safety and, at any rate, the JAL gimmick underlines Hochschild's hypothesis about control of emotional labour by airline managements.

Maybe JAL was trying to haul itself out of loss-making by inducing cabin crew with average salaries of 8 million yen to retire early and replacing them with contract crew who cost less than half - the 'resource' aspect of human resource management. Air hostesses on a year's contract with All Nippon Airways were similarly paid only 50 per cent of staff rates. The enterprise union accepted the cost-cutting policy because it protected most jobs at the company, although some took voluntary redundancy. One air hostess was reported as enjoying the job, even though there was no guarantee that she would become permanent and the low pay was a worry. 'It's a very happy company and a smile is part of our training.' (Harper, 1996).

The Customer as Champion

Despite the 'Putting People First' and 'Managing People First' programmes of the 1980s, not all of BA's operations were equally affected by the Total Quality Management approach. Surprisingly, these included customer relations. The new management team brought into customer relations subscribed to W. Edwards Deming's views that merely satisfying customers is not enough to retain their business and customer retention is crucial. As Deming put it, "profit comes from repeat customers - those that boast about the product or service". (Deming, 1988:178).

The method chosen was of making customers into champions, that is to say, loyal customers who would be active in providing BA with accurate information on the quality of its services. To champion the customer, the new management team instituted four objectives. The first was to use customer feedback more effectively in order to improve the quality of the airline's service. The second objective was to strive to prevent future service problems through teamwork. Line managers joined customer relations for monthly reviews of customer perceptions of service quality and quality improvement teams were continued.

> The bottom line became preventing customer defection. It was translated into a *modus operandi* of retain, invest, prevent, which was incorporated into all training programs, coaching sessions and performance criteria. Finally, the success of the customer retention strategy required partnerships with customer relations' internal customers - colleagues in other BA departments. Only with such partnerships could BA move from cure to prevention, utilizing the information collected by customer relations to design out service failures and to design in early warning mechanisms to

> pinpoint potential service failures, reducing the need for customer relations to act as a safety net. (Weiser, 1995:114-116)

That was all very well but seemed to fall by the wayside when strategy shifted to efficiency gains by sub-contracting and cost-saving. After the resultant strike, customer service training declined woefully.

Conclusion - Human Resource Management and Relations with Customers

Product and service quality are intimately intertwined. Quality service is not merely a question of getting front-line staff to behave impeccably in every one of their hundreds of daily customer contacts – Carlzon's 'moments of truth'. Rather, every aspect of the product and service must be designed, produced and delivered correctly, every time and *ad infinitum*. The managements of BA and other major airlines have found that the people-intensity of a service makes its quality far harder to sustain than that of a product. Airlines must adopt more of the measurement and research techniques that are available to transform many intangible aspects of a service into tangibles. By measuring constantly every customer - and employee - attitude, BA has done a more professional job than most. With the management's realisation that ignorance is not bliss, BA showed that the lack of comparative data to measure and benchmark operating performance need not be a problem. 'If the information does not exist, create it', said Sir Colin Marshall when he instituted BA's marketplace performance unit in 1983. (Prokesch, 1995:108).

A Sceptical Note on Customer Care

Despite all the talk about customer care and the huge volume of managerial discourse devoted to it, there still seems to be a discrepancy between the rhetoric of customer service and what many of us actually experience. There is a well-known chain retailing electrical goods where local staff often refuse to replace faulty goods. Everybody has endured the elaborate voice mail systems that involve lengthy delays. The author has recently experienced damage to hold baggage during a short-haul flight from Paris to Birmingham with only cursory attention to putting this right after very polite requests. This, occurred only a week after having completed a questionnaire on customer care for the same company during the outward flight.

There is a danger that the plethora of management books on quality will lead to a preoccupation with gimmicks. A survey by the Institute of Management (Benbow, 1994) reflected this by its statement of the obvious: 'Customers want the best quality at the lowest price.' Well, if wishes were horses, beggars would ride. Without denying the very real improvements in customer care that the previous paragraphs described, neither they nor the damage to baggage are reflected in the 1998 Egon Ronay survey of transatlantic airline services.

A team of under-cover inspectors travelled economy class and set out to assess the quality of the total in-flight experience, i.e. a measure therefore of the extent of Total Quality Management. Companies were assessed using nine criteria - queueing time at check-in; efficiency; comfort; friendliness; in-flight service; food; entertainment; the pilot's in-flight comments and the state of the lavatories. The results were mixed with the assessors summarizing by saying that they were surprised at the poor conditions and discomfort in economy class redeemed only by the friendliness of the majority of in-flight staff and the sometimes good in-flight entertainment. (Thorpe, 1998).

How Ronay's Inspectors Ranked the Airlines:

Airline	*points*
Virgin Atlantic	66
KLM	64
Continental	59
Air France	58
US	58
Delta	57
United	55
British Airways	51
American	48
Northwest	47

A further indication of customer satisfaction may be derived from responses to a questionnaire survey on travel among readers of *The Guardian* and *The Observer*. The top five airlines for leisure travel were

Emirates; Singapore Airlines; Thai; Air New Zealand and Virgin. For business travel, the five top-rated were Virgin Atlantic; Lufthansa; Scandinavian Air Services; British Midland and EasyJet, demonstrating that low-cost airlines are taking a share of the business market.

To the sceptic, what Total Quality Managment sometimes boils down to in the end is empowerment of responsibility at the point of service to 'make do and mend' for basically inadequate or inappropriate service quality. It cannot possibly be the case that the best quality at the lowest price is always meaningful. More sensible is Sir Colin Marshall's rejoinder that competing on cost and price is flawed: 'Compared with international flying anyway, the flying experience in the United States today is pretty ghastly. We've conducted extensive research with US Air and have very strong indications that many people in the United States are willing to pay a premium not to be treated like cattle.' (Prokesch, 1995:102). This point of view seemed to be substantiated by legislative proposals to increase passengers rights in the USA. A common feature of such proposals appears to be the request for 'more honesty from the airlines, both about the exact journeys passengers will be taking - owning up, for example, when a code-share flight is being operated by another carrier not shown on the ticket – and about what is going on when problems arise.' (Usborne, 1999) A study of all nine major US air carriers found that overall service quality had declined over the past 20 years and that airlines were concentrating their efforts on more lucrative first- and business-class passengers. (Rhoades & Waguespack,1999).

TQM policies contributed to BA's above average performance in the first half of the 1990s. The change in leadership unfortunately coincided with an attempt to secure yet more competitive advantage from cost-cutting with adverse results for service quality. Moreover, curiously, in the name of marketing and branding, a bizarre policy was adopted in 1998 that did not help the fading fortunes of the airline as competitors improved their service, applying their own versions of TQM. This sprang from the senior management wish to symbolize organizational change and identity change as part of the global strategy:

> Two years ago, BA had it all. A huge route network, a modern fleet united by a very strong image that contributed powerfully to positive corporate karma. The feelgood factor was tangible. And then someone did something unbelievably stupid. They did some research. They found that 60 per cent of BA's business originated outside the UK and inferred that patriotic identity was not necessarily appropriate. The BA research was applied top to bottom. It was suggested that with increasing deregulation

and new strategic alliances, the number of ethnically British passengers would inevitably drop below 40 per cent. The argument therefore developed that, since BA is a global brand, there was no need to have the union flag, or a version of it, on the tailfin of the aircraft. (Bayley, 1999)

This was a disastrous move right in the middle of a dispute with ground staff and cabin crews after senior management announced contracting-out of catering and ground staff employment and revised terms for pay, including consolidation of overtime and allowances and cuts for rates paid to new recruits. Popular indignation was expressed by John Kay in the *Sun*: 'British Airways chiefs are blowing £60 million on making tiny changes to their logo, while axing 10,000 workers to save costs. Three years later, at the first annual shareholders meeting after the Ayling era, the announcement that the ethnic designs would be removed was greeted with clapping and cheering. Lord Marshall, the BA chairman, said that new aircraft and those coming in for repainting would carry the old-style union flag design.

2 Relations with the State and Human Resource Management in Airlines

Relations with the state are a crucial determinant of human resource management processes and outcomes in the airline business. The main form of such relations used to be through public ownership. However, although many European Union carriers remain publicly-owned, this is no longer the norm.

> Enthusiasm for privatization within the European Union has produced efficiencies at formerly moribund flag carriers like Lufthansa – although Air France remains a notable exception to the rule. (Brummer, 1995)

By 1998, this was no longer the case, profitability at Air France had improved so that the French government could contemplate reducing its holding from 95 per cent to 53 per cent. In December 1999, BA bought a 9 per cent share in Iberia, paying £160m for a 9 per cent stake as one of seven corporate investors who agreed to acquire 40 per cent, the rest floated by a public share offer. The huge state-owned South African transport group, Transnet, is undergoing restructuring in preparation for privatization. Accordingly, a stake of 20 per cent in South African Airways (SAA) was sold to Swissair in 1999, with an option for a further 10 per cent. In the Asia-Pacific region, Thai International and Malaysian Air Systems are partly publicly-owned and Garuda (Indonesia) is fully publicly owned. There has been partial privatization in India.

However, even where airlines are privately owned, relations with the government - or, more accurately, with the national government and governments of other countries - are significant for management of their human resources. A completely deregulated or 'open skies' policy is inconceivable. Airlines need airports and landing rights at those airports.

In the field of international aviation policy, states are not normally concerned about the commercial aircraft of other nations flying through their airspace; their primary concern is with aircraft that want to make landings in their territory for the purpose of setting down and picking up commercial traffic. What is normally called 'the right to fly', might better be called 'the right to land'. (Wheatcroft 1964 : 68)

If an airline wants to expand into other markets, for instance to pursue a strategy of globalization - which was the espoused strategy of BA in the 1990s - landing rights are obviously indispensable. Basically, these can be obtained in two ways: one is for the national government of the country where the airline that wishes to expand has its head office to bilaterally negotiate with the government of the country where it wants landing rights. State authorities 'create' international airline routes by obtaining and granting 'rights to fly', through a series of agreements with other states. They negotiate for rights to fly routes *on behalf* of their own national airlines, giving away as little as possible to other national airlines. This puts the state authorities in a powerful position vis-a-vis their national airlines. They are in a position to alter the course of negotiations either indirectly by procedural means or directly by deciding whether to negotiate or not. In 1946 delegates from the United Kingdom and the United States met in Bermuda to negotiate bilaterally the exchange of commercial rights between their countries and this air services agreement has been periodically re-negotiated since.

A second way is simply to takeover the landing rights of another airline company. Possibly the opportunity may arise if a company has gone out of business and vacated landing slots, as was the case with Pan Am's landing slots in the late 1980s, those at Heathrow going to United. More likely, direct takeover or merger can acquire necessary landing rights and routes. BA did so when taking over the ailing Dan Air in 1992, acquiring its routes and landing rights at Paris and other European cities.

To varying degrees, national airlines can, of course, put pressure on their governments to take a more protectionist line over foreign investment, mergers and takeovers. In 1996 BA had proposed an alliance with American Airlines – somewhat surprisingly, given the vociferous opposition of Robert Crandall, then chairman of American, to BA's previous tie-up with US Air. However, rival airlines, such as United and Delta, were able to jointly lobby against the alliance by urging the US government to make an anti-trust inquiry. In August 1996 the proposed alliance was set back after US government officials withdrew from the next round of 'open skies' negotiations with UK counterparts, accusing the British government of shifting its negotiating stance at the last minute.

Talks on the transatlantic agreement that must accompany any BA/AA alliance had been going on for years. One sticking point was on 'beyond rights' to enable US carriers to fly from British airports to other European destinations; yet the right of UK carriers to operate domestic US services seemed to always be resisted, as was any commitment to easing US restrictions on airline ownership. In September 1996, Robert Crandall hardened and threatened to pull out of the proposed alliance if open skies talks went on for much longer. He said that he was neutral about a deal being agreed but made it clear that US pilots would never agree to British carriers being allowed onward access in the USA because of the threat it posed to US jobs.

By 1998, the European Commission had decided to approve the alliance, on condition that BA gave up some 250 of its slots at Heathrow to ensure access for competitors, such as Virgin and British Midland. This might have allowed London and Washington to try to complete negotiations on an agreement to liberalize transatlantic air services – though the EU Commission had also ruled that such bilateral deals contravene EU law. Not that this signified much because such open skies agreements had already been reached between the USA and the Netherlands - heralded as a model for future aviation agreements in 1992 – and with Germany in 1996. In January 1998, the Japanese and US governmental airline authorities approved an open skies agreement between United and All Nippon Airways, giving United onward cargo-carrying rights in Japan. Clearly this deal has employment implications for airline workers in Japan and was therefore roundly condemned by Japan Air Lines management.

Hence the US government negotiators were old hands at these bilateral agreements, having signed 31 of them, and expected the agreement with Britain to follow the same formula. However, the British negotiators were well aware that access to Heathrow is worth more than space on the apron at any other airport in the world. Certainly it is much more valuable than access to Frankfurt, Paris or Amsterdam. For that reason, they want to cut a special deal with the US. The UK wants to raise the issue of cabotage – the right of UK carriers to operate domestic US services – and to get a commitment from the US to ease restrictions on airline ownership. Given what is at stake – and the bargaining chip that the UK has in its grasp – it seemed worth playing the long game.

In October 1998, negotiations over open skies again broke down when US negotiators again walked out of the talks. Then the US Department of Transportation abandoned plans to hold a final round of hearings on the BA/AA alliance. Since clearly approval for the alliance and the signing of an open skies agreement were interdependent, BA's financial position was also crucial. Both the Clinton administration and the EU regulators were calling on BA and American to open the market to other airlines at the same time – just as BA's profitability had slumped and growth forecasts for the transatlantic market were being scaled down. As Chris Tarry, aviation analyst at Dresdner Kleinwort Benson put it: 'There is no point in going ahead with the alliance if it is going to hurt like hell. If traffic was still growing at 8 per cent, it would be fine but at between 1 and 3 per cent it becomes questionable. BA could end up doing itself a great deal of damage by inviting more competition in. It might be prudent and sensible not to go ahead with the alliance now.' (Harrison, 1998).

In January 2000, negotiations were resumed but soon broke down again. It was reported that the US negotiators were outraged when Britain refused to make concessions on opening Heathrow to more airlines. It was widely believed that BA had made representations to the British government. Consequently, it was indicated that the BA/American code-sharing agreement might be ruled uncompetitive. In March 2000, the US Department of Transportation denied Virgin Atlantic continuing access to Chicago. 'The pleadings in this case have raised foreign policy issues that cannot be reolved this time or in this context.' This short-term decision would 'provide us with the opportunity to reach a judgement on the merits in this case that provides the greatest public benefits and promotes our aviation objectives most effectively', stated the Department of Transportation. The move was interpreted as exemplifying the sourness of relations between Washington and London after negotiations over the new air services agreement broke down. (Marshall, 2000). When negotiations resumed in June 2000, Virgin Atlantic urged the UK government not to 'sell out' by accepting a one-sided deal with Sir Richard Branson quoted as saying 'if the British government caves in – which we are concerned they will, in return for US approval for a BA-American alliance – then we will have absolutely no leverage whatsoever to open up the domestic American market'. (Harrison, 2000). BA's planned takeover of KLM attracted the jealousy of rivals and opposition from US government officials who pointed out that if KLM came under BA control, it would be deemed to be subject to the aviation agreement made with the UK, not the treaty made with the Netherlands.

Henri Wassenbergh, onetime aviation legal specialist and adviser on international relations to KLM, described globalization as a myth and deregulation as a mistake.   What actually happened to BA's espoused global strategy – never consummated during the 1990s, despite considerable investment, suggests he may well have been right about globalization, given the absence of a supranational authority for controlling the development of air service and the tendency for national governments to give away as little as possible.   Even inside Europe, international air traffic control procedures are difficult to co-ordinate.   The problem is less technical than political.   In 1993, there were over fifty control centres with some 30 different systems, supplied by 18 computer manufacturers with over twenty different operating systems in over 70 programming languages.   Consequently, the European system is complicated, expensive to manage and inefficient.   The European Commission seeks to harmonise but national governments are reluctant to give up sovereignty over their skies.   Commercial interests mean that each country would like its own version to be the model for Europe's harmonized system.

Technology is now being developed to improve communications between aircraft and air traffic controllers.   In effect, pilots will take on more of the decision-making , thereby freeing airspace that was previously out of bounds owing to aircraft navigation and separation rules.   The aim of Eurocontrol, the 28 country organization that co-ordinates Europe's air traffic control planning, is for a new European Air Traffic Management System.   Again, it is claimed that 'one of the benefits is to reduce the workload on air traffic controllers by enabling pilots and computers to share the burden of traffic management'. (Tieman, 2000).

Whether deregulation will prove to have been a mistake is more questionable.   Its extent may be questioned, for example in Japan where opening to more international competition was concluded under great pressure.   Moreover, other Asian governments, probably partly mindful of the employment implications, have approached deregulation rather tentatively, as considered in the closing sections of this chapter.

Nevertheless, on the inauguration of the European Single Market, the European Union's third package of air travel deregulation measures came into effect.   Most importantly, European airlines were permitted to fly 'consecutive cabotage' so that any European Union airline serving a foreign destination gained the right to pick up traffic there and to carry it to a second destination in that country.   For example, BA flying from London to Frankfurt could pick up traffic in Frankfurt and carry it onto Berlin.   However, this was restricted to fifty per cent of overall seasonal capacity until April 1997. Full cabotage, or the right of any airline to fly freely inside another EU country was also delayed until April 1997. France, in particular, negotiated some procrastination.

A further element of deregulation related to national carrier licensing in that national ownership criteria is replaced by EU rules allowing EU countries to set up airlines in any of the EU countries. This may lead to the establishment of new foreign subsidiaries or cross-ownership on the lines of BA's purchase of a 49 per cent stake in the French regional airline TAT. (Smithers, 1993). BA bid for another smaller French state-owned airline, AOM, in October 1998. It faced competition from Lufthansa, Virgin Express, Swissair and Air France.

Though Air France management was stung by this yet further invasion of its traditional territory, it could not do much as an EU court had ruled in June 1998 that the EU Commission had been wrong to approve a F.fr 20 billion rescue subsidy in 1994. The EU Transport Commissioner's office responded that there was no question of Air France having to pay back the money while the Commission was deciding what action to take but there was clearly little realistic chance of Air France bidding for AOM.

In May 1994 a European Commission report had called for further changes to the airline industry in Europe, arguing for privatization and an end to government subsidy. Dan White, an airline analyst with National Securities, commented that, although deregulation in Europe would be 'pretty ferocious - plenty of blood would be spilt', the report did not mean open skies in Europe and this was not likely because the vested interests working against that were simply too strong. (Buckingham, 1994). Some EU carriers remain government-owned. They enjoy a regime whereby they operate on behalf of - and are finally supported by - their governments. They see their very survival threatened if the steady infusion of state aid which has kept them aloft for so long is withdrawn. However, the economic climate through the 1990s was in favour of privatization. Even the managements of Iberia and Olympic were prepared for this objective and were willing to countenance other airlines holding equity stakes in their companies.

The biggest barrier to deregulation or, more accurately, open competition, in the European Union is the idea that every member state has to have its own airline. The preconception that flying is glamorous or prestigious can again be questioned if air travel is so popular that airlines are just glorified bus companies. It was clear in 1994 that the contraction of the airline industry in Europe was inevitable but national governments were trying to make sure that when the battle came, their national carriers would be among the survivors. Consequently the Commission had little choice but to accept additional state equity for Aer Lingus of £150 million; £2.4 billion for the bankrupt Air France; £723 million for TAP of Portugal and £147 million from the Greek government to Olympic. The restructuring that was made a condition of approving the aid to Aer Lingus did establish a precedent that was again utilised in the case of Air France. However, when challenged by BA and others on competitive grounds, this argument of rationalization did not cut much ice with the European Union Court of First Instance which ruled that the state aid should not have been approved by the European Commission. (Ramesh, 1998).

The episode would appear to support the claim that 'a major motive behind the emergence of the subsidy morass is the attempt by governments to preserve jobs and slow the pace of economic adjustment in dealing sectors of the economy. The greater the extent and duration of these governmental measures, the smaller will be the relative valuation that employees and unions will put on job security provided by firms through explicit or implicit agreements'. (Burton, 1979). Confidence in a company's management of human resources is reduced by public measures of protection.

At Air France, Christian Blanc acted to change the allegedly bureaucratic culture of employees and improve the quality of service from 1995. This necessitated reform of working practices and terms of employment. He also appointed Jean-Pierre Courcol, a former publishing executive, as managing director of Air Inter, the domestic carrier. Responding militantly to the renewed restructuring and Courcol's appointment, SNPIT, one of the airline's biggest unions, described the move as a gross provocation and accused M. Blanc of concentrating power in his own hand. Partly due to the efforts of Christian Blanc, after years of losing money, Air France made a profit for the second half of 1997. However, he resigned in September 1997 in frustration at the government's unwillingness to accept his plan for full privatization. The intervening industrial relations climate is discussed fully in chapter 7. The government's alternative plan was to divest itself of part of the airline, leaving it with 53 per cent. Another 23 per cent was to be held by employees and the rest by investors and Air France's linked state-owned companies, guarding against the risk that its stake might drop below 50 per cent should Air France swap equity with another airline in an alliance.

Aer Lingus - New Industrial Relations Structure

An obvious difficulty with restructuring and the necessary cost savings plans that managers have had to implement at state-owned airlines is that the human resource management environment is liable to sharply deteriorate as concessions are demanded of unions and employees, despite – or possibly because of – improving profitability. An example of this was at Aer Lingus, particularly in respect of cabin crew and pilots. In an effort to improve matters, a new partnership-based industrial relations framework was negotiated by management and unions in 1997. The new framework involves a business group that passes information to a joint union/management partnership steering group. The procedure seemed to consist of negotiation in the normal way but, if necessary with the conciliation services of Ireland's main conciliation agency, the Labour Relations Commission. A final stage would be for issues to be considered by an internal tribunal chaired by an independent third party. This seems a bit over-constitutionalized but it may be better than BA's solution of *ad hoc* recourse to mediation to settle the pilots dispute in 1996. The Aer Lingus partnership framework entails an explicit recognition that restructuring and privatization is complex, as in the case of its sell-off of TEAM, its aircraft maintenance subsidiary, an issue that is discussed in chapter 6.

State Ownership Elsewhere

Few governments these days look kindly on arguments that national prestige justifies an airline's being unprofitable. Almost certainly this does not apply in the case of France but the unions were able to appeal to the state shareholder to provide the means to redress the situation. Moves to rationalise Lufthansa begun in 1992 were inspired by the determination of airline and German government to make the business pay. Jurgen Weber determined to stand with BA, KLM and SAS in opposing state subsidies to rivals with weak balance sheets and by 1999 Lufthansa costs per seat were falling and profitability rising to a far better performance than BA or Air France.

An extreme case where the state's ownership crucially affects human resource management is shown in Thai International Airways. Until government technocrats, (who wanted the airline to be more professionally managed), intervened in 1992, the airline had been controlled by air force officers with few business qualifications. Most of the 500 pilots of Thai nationality were former air force personnel.

Some airlines cross-subsidize internally by making revenue from profitable routes finance losses on unprofitable routes. Government policy may well dictate this inefficiency with the aim of national economic development. Garuda obtained a government guarantee to purchase planes in 1999 to carry out its mandate to link Indonesia's far-flung islands. Partially privatized in 1992, Philippine Airlines remains one third owned by the government. Domestically, it has the consequent built-in human resource management problems that were once prevalent among the state-owned airlines of Asia. Rigid fare controls meant that local services were unprofitable as PAL set the lowest fares in the world, after China. The result was that each Fokker 50 round trip flight from Manila to Baguio lost money at fares that would need a passenger load of 140 per cent of capacity to break even. When the airline was fully state-owned, 60 per cent of domestic routes were subsidised from international revenues but the privatized airline's management began to correct these inefficiencies.

To pursue this improvement, a new management structure was instituted in 1996. The Philippines Supreme Court threw out a petition from disgruntled minority shareholders who sought to restrain Mr. Tan, a prominent Chinese-Filipino businessman from taking majority control of the airline. Next, the Philippine Securities and Exchange Commission lifted its restraining order on the recapitalisation of PAL. Consequently, Jaime Bautista, chief financial officer at PAL, reckoned that the airline could be modernised: 'We will be able to raise capital abroad, rationalise the workforce and give PAL a new image.' (Luce,1996). Plenty needed to be done. With a workforce of 14,000 and strongly unionized, PAL was overmanned and continuously troubled by industrial disputes. Bautista estimated that personnel would have to be cut by 20-50 per cent.

On the domestic routes where poor performance accounted for about 30 per cent of PAL's losses, reform was more difficult, given the regulated 38 provincial destinations and Bautista admitted that the management was lobbying the government to change the regulations but without much optimism. Part of the problem was that PAL's three new competitors - Cebu Air, Grand Air and Air Philippines – can cherry-pick the most profitable routes without the attendant obligations.

> We are confident that with our experience we can beat off our new rivals. We would appreciate a little more understanding from the government, though. (Luce, 1996)

Sadly, the restructuring plans proved over-optimistic and by late 1998, PAL was on the verge of collapse, although the government agreed to spend \$33m to keep freight operations and domestic routes operating for another month.

A dose of privatization in India was thought likely to lead to a sorely needed improvement in the performance of Air India. Officials portrayed the government decision of January 1997 as an 'open skies' accord that would deregulate, reinvigorate and modernize India's languid air travel industry. However, as foreign companies were allowed to hold up to 40 per cent equity in Indian carriers as long as the investors were not airlines or airports, it appeared that the government did not want aviation expertise. The effect was to keep the market closed to the proposal by Singapore Airlines and the Tata Group for a joint venture airline and apparently to insulate Indian Airlines from competition. The implications for Jet Airways, India's most successful private carrier, were not clear. Jet's chief executive, Nikos Kardassis responded that they were 'just as confused as everyone else. The policy seems to change every week'.(Karp, 1997). There was a renewed privatization program announced in April 2000 but a sense of *déjà vu* as the government ruled out foreign purchases of Indian Airlines or Air India. In practice, this would be likely to mean no bids from airlines at a time when neither Indian carrier was able to compete in an expanding market. As Murasoli Maran, the commerce and industry minister rather whimsically put it: 'For sentimental reasons, we can't allow foreigners to buy our airlines.' (Gardner, 2000).

In general, most state subsidies to airlines are justified by arguments about national prestige and national interest. This clearly conflicts with the general ban on state aids in the European Union, according to the Treaty of Rome. The obvious rationale of such a ban is the political imperative to render the opening of borders - dismantling protection in a single market - acceptable to member states. Only if a member state can be sure that its companies do not have to compete against the resources of other member states' governments will it accept integration.

To this end, the European Competition Commission has gradually established guidelines covering the legitimacy of state aids to industry. The airline business has proved particularly difficult to control and human resource management has proved a significant factor. Air France's huge subsidy was contested at the European Court of Justice by BA. However, it has to be remembered that the Commission made approval of the subsidy subject to conditions, including acceptance of BA's entry into Orly airport via its stake in TAT that Air France had been compelled to divest in 1990 by the then Competition Commissioner, Sir Leon Brittan. Despite other conditions, including a prohibition on fleet expansion, for the first time other national airlines, BA, KLM and Lufthansa, vigorously opposed the subsidy. In 1995, Neil Kinnock's first big task as the new European Transport Commissioner appeared to be to ensure that thousands of Iberia Airlines employees lost jobs. As in the Air France case, the unions were going to complain that if he blocked the aid there would be massive redundancies - yet, according to the guidelines, the aid could only be allowed on condition that it was accompanied by a plan to return to profit that would necessitate job cuts. In December 1994, about 70 per cent of Iberia staff had voted for a scheme designed to cut costs and increase competitiveness through gradual lay-offs. Harsher measures were to be applied unilaterally against the pilots who had refused the plan because they would have to bear the brunt of the salary cuts. Their reaction generated brusque condemnation and was seen as a selfish move by a relatively overpaid group that threatened the airline's future.

3 Relations with Investors, Suppliers, the General Public and Competitors and Human Resource Management

Discussing traditional personnel management, there would be little necessity to consider employee relations with respect to investors, suppliers, the general public and competitors. However, the usual definition of human resource management as aspiring to a strategic approach to the management of employment in the organisation opens all these areas to the legitimate interest of employee relations.

> Under economic changes strategic human resource management would include changes in markets, or market segments, changes in competition (new entries, takeovers, decline), changes in the national or local economy in terms of inflation rates, unemployment, interest rates and balance of trade. (Mabey, Salaman & Storey 1998:26)

Human Resource Management and Relations with Investors

In the case of publicly-owned airlines, this relationship follows closely on what was discussed in the previous chapter. Loss-making state-owned airlines managements have searched for economies and job cuts that their governments made the price of continuing subsidy. As the Air France case shows, this can leave the human resource management looking alternately macho and bullying - if management prerogative is stressed and compulsory redundancies proposed - or, completely ineffectual if union demands are conceded. Strike action was immediately in the public area and visible, creating dreadful publicity and adding millions each day onto the balance sheet that by any normal commercial standards reflected bankruptcy. The unions' and employees' expectations were for state intervention. In calling the strike of all Air France employees in November 1992 the 14 unions also appealed to the state shareholder to provide the necessary means to redress otherwise irreconcilable differences resulting from planned job and pay cuts. They were not unaware that the government had bolstered Air France with a 2 billion franc cash injection and 1.2 billion franc stake from BNP, before its privatization. Although management responded that the time has passed 'when the solution to problems of Air France could be found elsewhere than at Air France'. (Laroniche, 1992) it was difficult to argue that the umbilical cord with the state had been cut when Air France remained nationalised. The following year, Attali's desperate move of proposing even higher job cuts led to rank and file-led strike action and demonstrations at Orly and Charles de Gaulle airports that led the government to yield, forcing Attali to withdraw the plan and to resign. His successor still had the problem of finding the 4000 job cuts - more slowly - as a further 20 billion francs of capital was offered by the government and approved by the European Commission.

Aer Lingus received a capital injection of nearly £75 million in 1993, with more to come in 1994. Some Aer Lingus losses stemmed from a policy pursued by successive governments that the airline should be a tool of regional policy by obliging all transatlantic flights to make a stop over at Shannon. The thousand job cuts so far seemed unlikely to satisfy the conditions attached to the state aid or to return the airline to profitability. More drastic rationalisation was obstructed by employees in the maintenance division, TEAM Aer Lingus, who held up servicing of aircraft following lay-offs. As a result, Virgin cancelled its maintenance contract. In late 1997 AER Lingus management were engaged in talks with prospective partners interested in investing in a majority stake in TEAM. Before any deal could be agreed, management had to negotiate an agreement with the unions to compensate a majority of TEAM's employees for relinquishing their legal rights as Aer Lingus employees.

Few governments these days are benign about supporting loss-making airlines. In 1993 the German government approved plans for the gradual privatization of Lufthansa. As a first step, the government reduced its stake from over 50 per cent to 38 per cent by not participating in a DM 515 million rights issue. The agreement on privatization was negotiated by management, the transport and finance ministries, the state pensions fund and the trade union. The problem of employee pension payments had obstructed privatization moves for years. The whole process was in marked contrast to the Air France impasse but helped by an anticipated return to profit and the first dividend to ordinary shareholders since 1989.

Privatization of Iberia was also assisted by its return to profit in 1999. Nevertheless, corporate investors, such as BA, negotiated the right to sell shareholdings back to the state holding company, Sepi, if full public flotation had not taken place by the end of 2000. BA and five Spanish companies paid half their combined investment of £700m in December 1999, with the balance due when the Spanish government cleared the sale. (Harrison, 1999). When BA declined to take up its option of a 20 per cent stake in Olympic, the Greek airline's board refused to pay the sum owed to Speedwing, a consulting subsidiary of BA, after abruptly terminating its contract. As discussed in chapter 7, Speedwing had been contracted to take over human resource management at Olympic. The apparently optimistic scenario could not overcome a dispute about Speedwing's handling of Olympic finances.

None of these European state airline relationships come anywhere near the effect on human resource management that has previously existed in the partially privatized Thai Airways International. For many years until 1992 when a reforming government ousted them, Thai Airways was controlled by air force officers with few business qualifications, though day-to-day operations were usually handled by civilian managers. An interim government, appointed by royal decree in 1992 to defuse the political crisis, moved to reduce the military's influence in business enterprises controlled by the state, including Thai Airways. The new board found it hard to return Thai to profitability - as it had previously creatively accounted its profit figures by selling aircraft and leasing them back. Morale among the 18,000 employees had been affected by the crash in July 1992 of a Thai airbus bound for Katmandu, and by disputes between supporters and opponents of the military inside the organisation. At that stage most of the 500 pilots of Thai nationality were former airforce personnel. (Mallet, 1992). In common with other south east Asian airline managements, that of Thai has been seeking alliance with western airlines in order to improve human resource performance. Negotiations were held with Lufthansa management in 1996 and Thai joined the Star Alliance in 1998.

Improved business strategy was apparently the rationale when it was announced in 1998 that the government-controlled main shareholder of Taiwan's China Airlines would sell at least half of its 71 per cent stake in the carrier. China Airlines management had been in negotiation with several airlines, including BA, about sale of shareholdings 'to forge strategic alliances to strengthen competitiveness'. (Springett, 1997).

One of the alleged benefits of privatization is that management and employees are kept efficient by risk-taking. There are, however, obvious downside risks for the investor with consequences for human resource management. Airline income has been squeezed at the same time as their costs are rising. The main problem is over-capacity, particularly on transatlantic routes. Geoff Miller, head of research at Brewin Dolphin Securities warned investors in June 1999: 'You have to be very careful of airline companies. They are very cyclical and they have to get their strategy right. Internationally, airlines have a history of not getting their strategy right and those that don't aren't there any more. They are traditionally an area where investors have had their fingers burnt and, at the moment, they will look at the way airfares are going and avoid the sector completely because they assume that you can't make any money flying people to Ireland at £40 a time.' (Root, 1999). For all that, Ryanair was the world's most profitable airline, with operating margins of over 20 per cent in 1999, healthier than the famous Southwest Airlines of the USA. US investors own 48 per cent of Ryanair and find the stock profitable enough to hold. According to chief executive Michael O'Leary, 'they love us because they understand the Southwest story.' (Brown, 2000). They may see a resemblance between O'Leary and Herb Kelleher. After pre-tax profits leapt from IR£12.1m (£9.5m) to IR£15.7m (£12m) in the final quarter of 1999, Michael O'Leary announced plans to create 250 'highly-paid' jobs for pilots and cabin crew in the UK as the group added new aircraft and launched new routes.

By contrast, managers of investor institutions, such as Mercury Asset Management (17 per cent of BA shares), had been highly critical of Robert Ayling for his handling of human resource management, especially during the industrial disputes of 1997:

> We won't move on him while the threat of dispute still exists but we will want to ask what he thinks he has achieved. Service businesses depend on the morale and goodwill of staff and they have the ability to jeopardize business in the longterm. (Buckingham, 1997)

Eventually, his resignation was forced as BA's losses mounted in early 2000. Shareholders were unforgiving and strongly criticized BA's £2.5m pay-off to the former chief executive. Lord Marshall, drafted in to take the flak, admitted that 'employee morale deteriorated along with the results and the situation was, as you know, reflected in the share price'. (Bentley, 2000).

In the proposed merger of BA and KLM in June 2000, a contentious issue was how the benefits of the merger would be shared between BA and KLM shareholders. The Dutch airline was apparently pressing for a 30 per cent interest in the combined business, even though it would receive only 15 per cent on the basis of the respective prices of the two companies' shares. 'For us and, no doubt, BA's shareholders, the benefits must be visible and more importantly, achievable, and in some areas these are not immediately obvious', stated a study by transport analyst Chris Tarry of Commerzbank.

Relations with Suppliers and Human Resource Management

The key issue here is how much to sub-contract. Without doubt, the emphasis in the last two decades has been on down-sizing and concentrating on core activities. One rationale has been to create a leaner staff and organizational structure. Although not exactly new, the model generally used to theorize about this was the core-periphery model. Here a leaner staff of permanent employees operates the core activity of producing arrivals of passengers and freight. Peripheral activities, such as catering and maintenance, may be sub-contracted to be carried out by other firms. As a precursor to privatization, Lufthansa's steps to reduce its activities to a core included selling off its airline catering subsidiary. Subsequently, the dismissal of 270 employees in Britain led to a seventeen month dispute.

Buyer-supplier relations are a crucial area for Total Quality Management. Simply using a policy of lowest offer tendering will cut costs but this may be once-for-all and potentially militates against quality, certainly against the long term perspective theoretically associated with TQM. Therefore a continuing relationship with suppliers is often recommended, with training and guidance as part of the network. BA's operation in catering had been a joint ownership operation with Trust House Forte but THF was taken over by Granada and BA management announced plans to sell the catering operation in 1997.

Whilst contracting should work satisfactorily for airline catering, maintenance is a different matter. The airline without its own maintenance facility is at a serious disadvantage that competitors will exploit. During the acrimonious commercial war between BA and Virgin, BA unceremoniously withdrew facilities that Virgin had been sub-contracting. Virgin was able to switch to Aer Lingus maintenance facility, TEAM, but at higher cost. Furthermore, this was ultimately unsatisfactory because

Virgin management had no control over the Aer Lingus human resources. Employees at TEAM were fighting job cuts and lay offs as Aer Lingus attempted to cut costs. They caused chaos by disruptions and working to rule so that Aer Lingus could not guarantee work schedules would be met. Virgin was obliged to obtain aircraft servicing from KLM.

The fundamental buyer-supplier relationship in the airline industry is that with aircraft manufacturers. Some airlines have attempted to spread the heavy fixed costs by means of aircraft leasing. It allows scope for some short term 'creative' accounting. However, during the recession of the 1990s, the huge growth that had taken place in leasing was seen to be something of a confidence trick that obscured the over-capacity in the industry and may have partly derived from public subsidy to the manufacturers, allowing them to supply below cost. Aircraft manufacturing directors were quite pleased when Guinness Peat's share flotation was a flop, hoping that more immediate pressure for airline rationalization would be exerted, thereby raising airline profitability and the ability to pay for new aircraft. However, such hopes were confounded by poor figures for Boeing in early 1995 as airlines continued to cancel and defer orders.

It might be thought that the fewness of aircraft manufacturers would give them more bargaining power in relations with airline companies purchasing aircraft. In fact, even as market conditions improved somewhat, the fierce competition among airlines induced them to put pressure on the manufacturers for concessions. In 1999 it was reported that Airbus Industrie was offering to buy back BA's fleet of Boeing 757s in an effort to induce BA to buy new Airbus aircraft. Such a part exchange could be seen as retaliation for a deal by Boeing to buy 17 Airbus A340 aircraft from Singapore Airlines in oder to induce SIA to convert options for 10 Boeing twinjets into orders worth $1.9 bn. Globalization and deregulation does not only have an effect employment relations and working conditions in the airlines but also among production, design and technical workers employed by Boeing and Airbus. In 1994 the chief executive of British Aerospace had warned that civil aircraft manufacturers would take an increasingly tough line with financially ailing airlines.

> It's no good going back to the investors or the equity markets for money to put into lousy airlines. Manufacturers will not support tupenny-ha'penny airlines in Chapter 11. (Beavis, 1994)

This reference to US bankruptcy relief for airlines, enabling them to stay in business, was obviously a misconception, however, as subsequent experience suggests that the aircraft manufacturing companies and their employees were better off with some degree of regulation. Back-biting between Boeing and Airbus continued in 2000 when Boeing management lobbied the US government against the proposed giant Airbus, citing unfair subsidised competition by the European airlines - a knotty point for competition lawyers.

Relations with the General Public and Human Resource Management

Increasingly through the last decade, public relations departments and agencies have been concerned with organizations' human resource management. Given the importance attached to image and corporate culture, perhaps this is not surprising. For example, it was widely acknowledged that BA failed to win the media battle about the strike of cabin crews in 1997 (discussed in chapter 7). As a result, Brunswick Public Relations was hired to play the PR role in any industrial relations problems.

In 1998, an investigation by the International Air Transport Association revealed that many had poor communications and were ill-equipped to deal with the public in the event of an accident. The main failings occurred among some of the larger US carriers, one of whose communications were described as 'very poor'. The IATA stated that many companies had cut their communications departments and crisis management techniques needed improvement.

Relations with Competitors and Human Resource Management

As explained in the opening chapter, competition is the driving force behind most recent changes in human resource management. It can lead to the most drastic consequences - redundancies. When Dan-Air was taken over by BA, Virgin Atlantic and British Midland failed in their High Court attempt to have the takeover investigated by the Monopolies and Mergers Commission. Previously, Virgin had negotiated with Dan-Air and then pulled back from merger and the £35 million BA takeover was probably the only alternative to liquidation that would have cost all 2,350 Dan-Air employees' jobs. However, as it was, BA found jobs for only 450 former Dan-Air employees. The takeover also caused problems for existing BA staff at Gatwick - 1,000 ground staff and 250 short travel cabin crew. They were offered jobs with the new organization only if accepting pay cuts of

30 per cent (and a one-off payment of a year's salary) - or early departure and severance pay. The staff voted overwhelmingly for a strike over the proposed pay cuts and changes in working conditions. For older airline crew of Dan-Air, the dole queue was a bitter reward for long service, while finding a job at a bleak time for the industry was difficult. One Manchester-based pilot, the captain of a Boeing 737, had been employed by Dan-Air for 15 years but received just the state minimum redundancy payment of £3,690 and five months pay in lieu of notice.

An older example is that of Texas Air Corporation (TAC), headed by Frank Lorenzo, who set up New York Air, a non-union carrier to challenge Eastern Airlines on its profitable Boston-New York-Washington route. The direct attack on Eastern led to its making losses and in 1986 TAC took it over. The new management then asked the unions for cuts in pay and benefits. When they refused TAC began to dismantle Eastern which ceased operations in 1991, leaving 18,000 employees facing an uncertain future. (Hinthorne, 1996).

These two cases suggest that we need to distinguish between short-haul and long-haul air transport in analysing the effect of relations with competitors on human resource management. When BA Speedwing took on responsibility for human resource management at Olympic and the unions threatened to hit local tourist flights, the immediate, self-defeating effect was on local bookings with Olympic. The entry into the market of price-cutting short-haul carriers has obviously affected human resource management in all continents. In Europe, the establishment of Go by BA as a short-haul competitive response to Easyjet and Debonair led to a 'beauty contest' when it came to union recognition. The GMB began a campaign to recruit employees of Go and other cut-price airlines in March 1998, despite 'disappointment' that other unions had decided to compete for members. 'When we recruit members at Go, it will be irrespective of any agreement reached by management with another union,' said Sean Keating, national officer of the GMB. (Clement, 1998). Taking advantage of the union rivalry, Go management wanted the successful union to agree to a three year pay freeze and for up to a third of employee pay to be performance-related. At least there was some degree of union recognition at Go. As discussed in Chapter 7, Ryanair refused to recognize unionization of baggage handlers in Ireland, insisting that its other employees were content with direct communications, leading to a bitter dispute and strike early in 1998.

Long-haul operators are generally seen as the predators in competition with companies, such as Ryanair that confine their market to short-haul. Like BA with Go and KLM with Buzz, many have tried to beat the low-cost carriers at their own game, having generally failed to drive them out of business by market dominance. According to Michael O'Leary, chief executive of Ryanair, this has enhanced the customer credibility of the sector: 'Go has been great for us. Before BA entered the field, all you had was Ryanair and EasyJet and there was a suspicion that we might be skimping on the maintenance. What's really brilliant about BA is that they spend millions advertising low fares but don't actually provide a lot of them. Long may it last. We like to compete with people who aren't any good and BA fits the bill perfectly.' (Brown, 2000).

Intensified competition among the giant carriers has not led to quite the degree of globalization that was anticipated. Transnational mergers have proved difficult and trying to avoid those organizational problems by non-merger agreements still tends to fall foul of the competition regulations of the USA and EU. Consequently, despite previous failures of alliances and co-operative ventures, these were again on the strategy agenda. Alitalia joined an alliance of KLM and Northwest (Wings), in the hopes of applying for anti-trust immunity and permission to market services jointly. This was to compete against the alliance of Lufthansa, United, Thai, SAS, Air Canada and VARIG of Brazil (Star) and Oneworld. The latter, an alliance of BA, American, Cathay Pacific, Canadian and Qantas, admitted a cost-cutting objective.

Managers of other airlines are sceptical about the alleged benefits of alliances. One thing is for sure – they potentially lead to very messy forms of competition – tinged with collusion - that are a certain benefit only for competition lawyers. When British Midland joined the Star alliance and planned to sell Lufthansa 20 per cent of its shares, BA management reacted strongly, contrasting the potential benefit to Lufthansa of British Midland's position at Heathrow – 24 per cent of landing slots (BA has 38 per cent) with the EU Commission's stern strictures about the abortive BA/American alliance.

> This re-opens the whole issue of our alliance with AA. It changes the ball game completely. Once upon a time there were vibrant British car and shipbuilding industries. Now they are foreign-owned and we can see that happening with airlines. There will be major carriers controlled from Fort Worth and Chicago and Frankfurt and there will be us, reduced to a niche player. (Harrison, 1999)

BA management's fear of the use of British Midland as a kind of Trojan horse to gain entry into Heathrow was further activated by proposals that would allow British Midland to start four daily services to the USA in return for a similar number of flights between two new US entrants to Heathrow. For once BA management was joined by Virgin, 'also opposed to seeing competition increase in the transatlantic market already plagued by overcapacity and falling yields'. (Done & Odell, 2000). Hence in the long-running negotiations about revision of the bilateral agreement between the UK and USA, BA asked the UK government to sideline any proposal to allow more airlines to operate out of Heathrow. It was prepared to see one airline, US Airways, given the Gatwick-Pittsburgh route but, in return, wanted US government acceptance of its alliance with American. In May 2000, British Midland disclosed that the British government had forced it to give an undertaking that it would not scrap any domestic UK routes in return for being granted the right to start transatlantic services.

It is a moot point whether the changing organization and strategy of airlines are forms of oligopolistic control, though they certainly involve collusion. The resort to strategic alliances and joint ventures perhaps depicts not so much market dominance as a response to technological and commercial uncertainties beyond individual company control. The managements are worried about costs because of deregulation and intense competition for market niches. It is very difficult for the majors to beat Southwest or Ryanair at their own game. Deregulation has encouraged airline managers to develop predatory management styles as a means of survival or to prosper and grow. 'Their intentions are to consume their competitors and to destroy any opposition to protecting and enhancing shareholder wealth.' (Hinthorne, 1996). The predatory management styles suggest that these managers' view of human relations has, as its frame of reference, a sociology of conflict. Any such 'sociology of conflict focuses on the distribution of power and relations of dominance. Radical change is seen as inevitable and manageable. (Dahrendorf, 1959). To achieve it – and enhance shareholder value – alliances are part of the mobilization of power in 'transitory relationships of unity, compromise and conflict as stakeholders manoeuvre for advantage'. (Hinthorne, 1996). In many of the examples of competitive moves discussed above, they are intended to create irreparable damage - and often do so – with unions undermined, jobs lost and salaries cut. It was hardly surprising, therefore, that the pilots' union at United Airlines voiced 'strong concern' about the proposed takeover of US Air by United in May 2000. Rick Dubinsky of the Airline Pilots' Association stated that he was 'deeply disappointed that the company would enter into a transaction of this magnitude without reaching full agreement with the United pilot group'. (Harrison & Usborne, 2000).

The take-over would create a global carrier with annual revenues of $25bn. and a fleet of over 1,000 aircraft serving more than 300 destinations, consolidating United's position as the world's largest airline. Not only that but the United-led Star Alliance would be strengthened – a challenge for other global airline groups and alliances. Hence, for a time that summer, the competitive situation of the airline industry resembled a diplomatic game of threatened competitive takeovers. The first response was a proposed bid of BA for KLM that would create the world's third biggest airline after United and American. There would be tough regulatory requirements, particularly how BA would acquire KLM's previously negotiated rights to fly to third countries in that these need to be agreed bilaterally between the national governments and, notoriously, the US and UK governments have failed to re-negotiate on several occasions. The indications were that if KLM came under BA control, it would be deemed to be subject to aviation treaties made with the UK, not Holland. Nevertheless, the prospect of a BA takeover of KLM was taken sufficiently seriously for Chris Tarry, transport analyst at Commerzbank, to carry out a study of its potential effects. He theorized that there would be 16,000 job cuts to achieve the cost savings that would commend the merger to shareholders. The bulk of these – 10,400 - would be borne by BA, compared with 5,800 at KLM. A further 3,200 jobs could be lost if BA were to withdraw from short-haul services at Gatwick and a reduction in the size of the long-haul fleet could result in another 4,000 job losses among the 98,000 combined workforce. Opposition from the KLM works council had helped repel a previous proposed merger of the two companies in 1992 and could be expected again, while staff morale and labour relations would be unlikely to improve at BA in such circumstances. (Harrison, 2000).

4 Airline Organization and External Relations

Dealing with excess capacity has been one of the main organizational problems for airline management. One approach has been through mergers which are often really disguised bankruptcies. However, mergers run up against the issue of national autonomy and sovereignty, and, though to a much lesser extent, possible restriction on anti-trust grounds. One way round this has been the creation of global alliances whereby two or more airlines continue as separate commercial entities but develop code-sharing arrangements so that there is some integration. It is curious that in an era of deregulation and intensifying competition, such collusion should be viewed as legitimate and even encouraged by governments.

There are now many global alliances among airlines. When BA's global strategy component of increasing its incursion into the US market by way of merger with United or KLM (through the latter's stake in North West) was thwarted, the management bought a stake in US Air. Although lobbying by United, American and Delta managers led the US authorities to restrict BA's stake, it nevertheless opened opportunities for code-sharing whereby US Air passengers could be fed onto BA transatlantic routes. Unfortunately, US Air was not exactly a popular consumer choice in the USA. Delta replied by reaching a code-sharing arrangement with BA's gadfly, Virgin Atlantic. However, this arrangement was frustrated by the lack of agreement between the British and US governments on liberalized air services, despite considerable lobbying in the USA on behalf of Delta/Virgin. Similarly, the BA/American alliance was undermined when the countries again failed to re-negotiate the Bermuda 2 landing rights agreement in January 2000.

Almost a decade earlier, KLM's management bounced back from fruitless merger negotiations with BA management by determining to develop its partnership with Northwest. The partnership had been hindered by US anti-trust laws and previous bilateral restrictions but the US and Netherlands reached an 'open skies' agreement in September 1992, allowing KLM to fly into any US city and US carriers access to any

Dutch destination. Elliot Seiden, Northwest's vice president, told the annual Commercial Aviation Authority conference in Washington DC that the two airlines could now expect 'an on-line service' that takes care of every stage of a passenger's journey. A key to the alliance's success is the emphasis on code-sharing, the system by which joint flights are given both KLM aand Northwest flight numbers. Seiden reckoned that no airline could realistically hope to grow by itself unilaterally into a complete global network. Both KLM and Northwest shared the vision of global network but through alliances,rather than internal growth. There were negotiations on a country-by-country basis for more such agreements between the USA and EU member countries but in March 1995 the Transport Commissioner swiftly ruled against any further deals of the KLM type. Moreover, when BA sought to merge with KLM, US Department of Transportation officials made it clear that KLM would be deemed to be subject to aviation treaties made with the UK.

Several alliances have been facilitated by mutual use of computerised reservation systems. The firepower of the Apollo and Sabre CRS in the USA alarmed Bernard Attali when he was president of Air France in the early 1990s, indicating the competitive advantage they gave to United and American. Consequently, Air France developed Amadeus in collaboration with Iberia, SAS and Lufthansa. CRS were now being transformed from rather limited flight reservations systems to production management and yield-management tools. Singapore International Airlines' marketing alliances with other airlines began in the 1980s through Swissair's CRS. By way of this connection, SIA became associated with Delta and the two companies agreed a share swap arrangement. Asian airlines can gain an advantage by arranging to match schedules with a US airline so that an SIA flight will connect conveniently with a large number of internal flights. Correspondingly, Delta secured outbound traffic from the USA to pass onto SIA. This partnership illustrates how 'CRS technology provides airlines with an almost infinite variety of means to respond to the needs of the various categories of customers'. (ILO:56). The arrangement transcends merely matching schedules to encompass mutual marketing so that both the airlines' connecting flights can share the same status in the CRS. The resultant prominence from this code-sharing in the CRS display will reflect both airlines' relative importance within the network and influence their revenue from the system. Moreover, the transformation of the CRS into a global information system enables the airlines to profit by developing end-to-end fares and packages, such as hotel check-in facilities, transport to and from the hotel and other services.

If, as many (though not all) managers in the industry suggest, it is due to become an arena of megacarriers, airlines that do not enter such cooperative arrangements risk being isolated. SIA subsequently agreed a second equity swap with Swissair.

Today CRS are an essential element in the airline business and in travel in general. In the USA an estimated 95 per cent of all travel agencies are linked to at least one CRS, 88 per cent of all airline tickets are issued through a CRS. All the main CRS encompass features that enable travel agents direct access to a participant airline's own database for real time bookings and reservations. At one stage to be successful, the CRS needed to be in touch with its customers - the travel agents. As travel agents became more global, the CRS had to become more global. The CRS enables the travel agent to provide a very tailor-made service by developing corporate customer profiles held on the CRS, for example detailing what company policy is on flight class or airline and the traveller's preferences. It has already been noted that CRS play an important role in what airline managers call 'inventory control' - or maximizing revenues from each seat. Airlines try every day to cut prices just enough to sell while keeping them high enough to make profits. The margin is thin. American Airlines reckoned that the marginal passenger on every flight adds $114 million to revenues.

At one stage it was predicted that

> it is more likely that competition will take place, not among individual airlines, but among CRS networks, and that an airline's prominence in the CRS display will reflect its relative importance within the network and determine its revenue from that system. (ILO, 1990:59)

Europe is already only part of the battlefield where large CRS operations are vying to build global systems. The rise of global industries and extensive international travel for business and pleasure has propelled CRS development. As travel agencies followed their customers overseas and formed international alliances, CRS have had to do likewise. Galileo International's chief executive emulated the dominant business strategic thinking of the time in saying that to be a successful CRS,

> you need to be in touch with your customers - the travel agents. As they have become more global, we have had to become more global. (Taylor, 1993)

We now seem to be emerging from an era in which travel agents utilized CRS systems that had been established by the big airlines. Those same airlines now do not see the point of losing a portion of potential revenue to travel agents. Although the last decade has been characterized by sub-contracting by large companies, e-commerce gives the airlines the chance to keep more revenue in-house by direct selling. Operations managers learned the advantages of the airlines developing their own customer profiles and direct online booking.

In the past

> there has been some concern about the possibility of the CRS industry becoming more and more oligopolistic or even monopolistic. In the operation of CRSs there are some very high fixed costs but marginal cost is close to zero. Hence there are some enormous economies of scale, with average cost declining continuously as the number of bookings dealt with increases. There may be no natural monopoly in airline operations but it is possible that there is one in CRS operations. There is no technical reason why global demand for CRS services cannot be met by one single mega-system. (Hanlon, 1996:57)

Concentration of economic power has increased somewhat in CRS markets. Sabre, formed by American Airlines, has the largest share of the US market. What Sabre management claimed to be the largest systems migration ever in the airline industry took place when some 200 US Airways information technology systems were shut down and their functions taken over by Sabre. Reportedly this entailed more than a million hours of combined planning and implementation by Sabre and US Airways employees. Hanlon noted that 'in 1991 negotiations took place between Amadeus and Sabre about the possibility of forming a marketing alliance, with Sabre taking an equity stake in Amadeus'. He commented that although this deal came to nothing, the structure of the industry was still evolving and might end up more oligopolistic than the airline industry itself.

There have been further mergers since 1995. Amadeus merged with System One of the USA. In the Asia-Pacific region, Sabre and Abacus combined to create Abacus International, using the Sabre system. Nevertheless, other competitive factors were developing that offset the apparent market power of the CRS. Firstly, 'with the exception of American Airlines' Sabre system, all CRS are now jointly owned' and multiple ownership encouraged the emergence of independent 'no host' systems that provide no preferential treatment for any one owner. As a result, 'CRS are becoming increasingly independent of their airline owners, operating more and more as businesses in their own right'. (Hanlon:58).

The CRS became learning organizations, both for their own employees and for the managers and employees of the parent airline companies. Many students of organizational learning, such as March and Olsen, Argyris, Schon, and, Simon treat organizational learning as individual learning in an organizational context. Others, such as Hedberg, Weick and Cyert and March, argue that organizations learn the same way as individuals learn. (Weick & Westley, 1997:441).

In Sabre, continual learning is emphasised as

> critical in helping Sabre stay at the leading edge of technology innovation. The Sabre website states that 'staying knowledgeable and taking ownership for self-development is important for every employee at Sabre. Our employees have the flexibility to seek out challenging assignments and have the opportunity to learn from the best in the industry. We encourage career planning, coaching and feedback through our formal performance management program. By concentrating on enhanced skills and learning new technology, our people are able to maintain their employability in the fast-paced technology industry. We have an extensive internal training department but also offer a tuition reimbursement program that allows employees to continue their education or to acquire training in specific skills that will open additional career opportunities. (Sabre, 2000)

In fact, entire organizations learn. The smaller airlines learned from use of the web to offer bargain prices to customers and fill short-haul flights to capacity, eliminating use of travel agents or very much reducing their role. 'Cutting out intermediaries such as travel agents is essential to achieving low prices for both Go and Easy-Jet. (Arthur, 1998). Smaller, low-fare airlines may try to avoid heavy distribution costs by direct booking and ticketless travel, now possible through automation, credit cards and the internet. As room for cost reductions in other areas was reduced and they joined in the cut-price competition with their own subsidiaries, the major airlines began to consider similar direct sales. Here the airlines learned from their use of CRS. Whereas, travel agents gained higher commissions on more expensive flights, CRS fees are charged on a per booking basis irrespective of the fare paid. Hence there was a big incentive for smaller airlines with higher proportions of low-cost fares to avoid them. However, there was also an incentive for the bigger airlines to go online. CRS generated an enormous volume of marketing data, enabling highly sophisticated yield management policies and elasticity of demand information.

> Because they have ultimate control of the seats, the airlines can also make their own offers if they want to sell off their seats at the last minute or drive traffic to their web sites by offering cut price fares. Lufthansa, American Airlines and Cathay Pacific have also run online auctions for tickets, some of which have sold at rock bottom prices. Travel agents who buy flight tickets in set price blocks, do not have the flexibility to use such techniques. (Payton, 1998)

Moreover, it can be argued that the growth of online booking in large companies is rather hindered by their traditional relationships with travel agents. Consequently, as part of a drive to cut costs in a market where it has been losing share to smaller and more nimble rivals, in January 2000 BA aimed to save money by abolishing the 7 per cent commission that it paid to travel agents.

> A percentage commission does not reflect the amount of work involved in a ticket sale. A more expensive ticket does not require a hundred times more work for the agent but it might attract a hundred times more commission. This new scheme is about working with agents better and more effectively but not just cutting costs. (Shah, 2000)

Nevertheless, it was an obvious conclusion that BA wanted its new payment structure to reflect the growing use of direct line payment for tickets, under which consumers obtain them over the telephone or internet from the airline, cutting out the agent. The next step was the establishment – in partnership with 10 other airlines – of an online travel agency offering customers the chance to compare up-to-date fare information and book flights directly. The site is to be managed independently of the airlines who include some of BA's fiercest competitors, such as Lufthansa, British Midland and Air France.

CRS continue to be important because they lend themselves to co-operation and joint ventures among groups of airlines, including national flagship airlines, because the participating airlines do not lose their separate identities and names, as they would in a merger. As a result, CRS technology enables airlines to transcend national and regional boundaries and to form international or global alliances. (ILO:59).

Joint ventures can also introduce a certain amount of collusion - with the usual effect of moderating competition. Lufthansa, Air France, Cathay

Pacific and JAL combined to develop TRAXON, a global communication network for the air cargo market, that went on-line in 1991. The system was intended to expedite computerised international cargo booking and offers all those concerned in the air freight business a rapid exchange of data worldwide. As in many other sectors of the globalized market, in the airline business joint ventures are increasingly important. As a Japan Air Lines manager put it in 1992, 'going it alone is too expensive'. Expense here does not refer only to the capital costs of installation. Airlines have conventionally made their forecasts and defined their strategies as individual companies. In such a cyclical and turbulent sector as air freight, they are coming to appreciate the potential advantages of collaborating and sharing information to produce a combined or global forecast of expected demand. DHL Worldwide Express uses its own airplanes for short-haul routes.For intercontinental flights it calls on leading airlines,including Lufthansa and Japan Airlines,with whom it has an alliance.The rationale of deregulation for policymakers in deregulating and opening markers to contestability runs up against the profit motive of international airlines.

However, joint ventures, like collusion, are naturally unstable. In October 1993, Swissair, one of four carriers concerned in a planned alliance - code named Alcazar - claimed that agreement was close. The agreement would have created a joint operating company with 400 aircraft and 70,000 employees. The following month negotiations collapsed as Austrian Airlines, KLM, SAS and Swissair failed to decide on which US partner would suit the alliance. Here previous alliances, such as that of KLM with Northwest, proved a hindrance, not a help.

In an industry with over-capacity and fierce price competition, alliances seem to offer advantages. On the formation of Oneworld, Anthony Tyler, director of corporate development for Cathay Pacific, was quoted as saying 'there is no future for an airline that is non-aligned.' (Bickers, 1998). Through the combined strengths that alliance can bring – shared premium services, such as lounges, code-sharing and corporate marketing – non-aligned airlines could be squeezed. On the other hand, Singapore Airlines, Cathay's biggest regional competitor, stayed away from the big alliances. As part of an alliance, if and when the Asian market started growing again, it could be questioned whether it would be SIA or alliance partners who gained most.

By May 2000 it was the Star Alliance, rather portentously self-styled 'the airline network for Earth', that seemed to be prospering the most. The biggest of the alliances, linking 800 destinations in 130 countries, there were 12 members, due to be increased to 14 by the addition of British

Midland and Mexicana Airlines. Moreover, the alliance seemed to be strengthened as a result of the takeover of US Air by its leading member, United – a challenge to every other global airline grouping, especially the Oneworld alliance.

PART II
INTERNAL RELATIONS

5 Theory of Airline Organization

Writing on airline management in the 1960s, W S Barry observed that 'an organization may be usefully regarded as distinct from the business that it serves. Not every business requires an organization for its success. Many sorts of businesses can be conducted with various forms of organization. Organization is something added and separable from business itself'.

This is a helpful observation in considering the business studies subjects of Organization Theory and Organization Behaviour. Organization Theory is mainly about organizational social structures, whereas Organization Behaviour is mainly about individual and group psychology, particularly for purposes of motivation. It goes without saying that these two subjects overlap. They may be reflexive, that is to say, critical of power subjects and how power is exercised. However, as management subjects, they are normally the servants of power, mainly reflecting managerial interests and doctrine.

> Organization is an instrument. It is an instrument used by a manager to achieve the intention of the head of the business. By definition, a manager is a person who acts through an organization. If someone commands and uses an organization, she should be regarded as managerial. Basically, the head of a business intends to sell something created by the process of changing what is already there (adding value). Her intention may or may not be achieved by the managerial use of organization. The managerial process involves the four major activities of planning, motivating, controlling and contracting. (Barry, 1965:89)

Planning

An indispensable part of managment is the notion of strategy. Undoubtedly, the usual definition of strategy encompasses medium and long term planning in the context of an enterprise's strengths, weaknesses, opportunities and threats. It begins with the question, 'what do we want to achieve?', generates a plan to achieve that intention and is then directed and divided for implementation in various parts of the organization.

Strategy, in these days of globalization and rapid market switches is frequently about the management of change and, consequently, nearly always involves human resources, as in Air France's strategic plan.

This rational view of strategy-as-planning has been subjected to trenchant criticism. Critics say that managers do not have sufficient information to plan, so that strategy is better seen as an incremental process or as emerging in the course of implementation and not at all separate from implementation. As in many other activities, the main problem is the difficulty in estimating the results of each alternative. Managers may justify investment decisions with sophisticated investment appraisal techniques but their sophistication does not diminish one iota the irremediable unforseeability of future returns and results. Even if we have an understanding of all variables affecting the business, it is impossible to be sure about predicting results. Demand for air travel seemed to be booming before Iraq's invasion of Kuwait and the consequent Gulf war led to a slump. Actually, the main variables affecting businesses are discerned only vaguely. 'There is no doubt about the truth of this proposition in the airline situation. Even if we were to identify all the variables at work in the airline situation, it would be impossible to predict their behaviour accurately because:

(i)   Certain situations can be foreseen on a statistical basis only. For example, it may be possible to forecast a percentage loss of aircraft through crashes but it will not be possible to forecast the day or month of the disaster.

(ii)   The airline situation is a competitive one. We can never be certain of the results of any plan because of the uncertainty of competitors' reactions to any move.

Having said this, we must remember that plans have more chance of being good if:

(i)   The variables in the airline situation are identified. The process of detection must therefore be continued unremittingly.

(ii)   The airline's knowledge of variables is kept up to date by taking into account the moves of competitors.

Because of the difficulty of estimating results, plan-changing becomes as important as plan-making and this should be reflected in the organization.' (Barry, 1965:90). That is, the organizational structure should be such that divisional managers can adapt plans to meet short term crises. Richard Pascale (1990:53) made much the same point when he wrote that 'there are, of course, instances in which strategic analysis played an important role in shaping a corporation's actions but, more often than not, strategic planning plays a secondary role in explaining the home runs that occur now and then. Many business breakthroughs result from an opportunistic response'.

Such plan changing can be illustrated by the changing fortunes of the strategies of BA and Air France. In the middle of the 1990s, BA was riding high, one of the few profitable international airlines and well embarked on a strategy of globalization. Air France, by contrast, was in the doldrums. Its CRS, Amadeus, developed with Lufthansa, Iberia and SAS, had proved costly to implement. The strategic plan, CAP93, intended to address weaknesses of low productivity and organizational inefficiency, had been obstructed by militant and effective industrial action which led to a climb-down and the resignation of Bernard Attali as chairman. BA had even invaded its domestic routes by the perfidious means of taking over the ailing Dan-Air, thereby gaining access to Orly airport, having previously purchased a 50 per cent stake in TAT, whereas Air France had been obliged to divest its holding. Ignominiouly, Air France's losses necessitated F.fr.20 billion in state aid and application to the Competition Commission for exemption from the anti-subsidy rules.

BA determined to consolidate its advantages by announcing a policy of further cost-cutting in its corporate plan. As discussed in chapter 7, however, there was strike opposition from the pilots in 1996 and cabin crews in 1997. It was extremely inopportune, coinciding with the row about the new logo. Moreover, having momentarily looked more promising than its abortive shareholding in US Air, the proposed merger partnership with American Airlines encountered delays from the EU and US regulators on competition grounds and eventually had to be abandoned. 'In effect, BA's international strategy was stalled for three years as competitors streaked ahead.' (The Economist,1999). Worse, the foray into Europe did not pay off as expected and Go, developed to contain competition from Ryanair and EasyJet, was struggling against them.

The transatlantic market, focus of the presumed benefits of the alliance with American Airlines, 'turned sour. Faced with a big fall in Asian business, many airlines switched their jumbos to the Atlantic. The ensuing price war cut revenues per seat over the Atlantic by about 10 per cent for the industry as a whole. BA's cost-cutting was a tactical response to all this and to a much-predicted downturn but it was to lead, somewhat serendipitously, to a strategy.' (The Economist, 1999). In 1997, management had to take an investment decision because the fleet of mainly 747s was due for replacement. Yield management revealed that a quarter of the seats on each jumbo were sold at below average cost. 'Hence the decision was taken to buy smaller wide-bodied jets for long-haul routes. Mr. Ayling spelled out his intention to shift his focus gradually from cut-price leisure travellers to the premium passengers from whom airlines make money.' (The Economist, 1999). In this third phase of post-privatisation development BA was increasingly turned into a business-class airline flying point-t-point passengers. According to Robert Ayling, this would make BA 'less dependent on transfer economy passengers where the yields are lower and the fares are not high enough to pay for the cost of the aircraft'. (Harrison, 1999).

By contrast, Air France was adding capacity, increasing its routes to the USA by means of alliances with Delta and Continental. When it was first planned, Air France managers were unhappy with the facilities at Roissy Charles de Gaulle airport. (Feldman, 1985:40). However, Bernard Attali's strategic move to sell its Montparnasse offices and relocate at Charles de Gaulle – central to becoming more market-led – can now be seen to have been justified. There is room for expansion and, by contrast with Heathrow, no strong opposition to more flights. True, Air France management encountered damaging strikes during 1997-1998 and the human resource strategy seemed no better than that of BA but perhaps growth permitted more room for manoeuvre. As further elaborated in chapter 7, the espoused strategy was one of incremental change, accepting the legitimacy of unions, the most militant of whom (the pilots), made a tactical error when they called a strike in 1998. Gallingly for BA, by late 1999, the Air France strategy seemed to be paying off with its operating margins improving to match BA's. Worse was to come for, shortly after BA reported its first loss since privatization, Air France reported net profits up by 42 per cent for the year to the end of March on a 14 per cent increase in revenues. It appeared that improving management-labour relations and declining government intervention (even though it remained 57 per cent state-owned) had helped it gain at the expense of its rival European carriers and the company was considering the purchase of ten A3XX superjumbos. The comparative fortunes of BA and Air France in terms of industrial relations are discussed in chapter 7.

Motivation

Motivation is conventionally treated as central to the study of organizational behaviour, not surprisingly in view of its importance for human resource management. Again, reflexively this may be criticised by adopting the point of view of subordinate employees who may feel alienated from the management's aims for the organization. It is a bit daft to interpret this as a lack of commitment on their part if they know that management strategy entails job cuts and more demanding working conditions for no more pay.

From management's point of view, however, motivation is central to Organizational Behaviour because it is concerned with getting things done in the (managerial) interest of the organization. 'In an airline this involves issuing a greater number of rules and regulations that tell people what to do and what not to do. It includes verbal and written instructions, temporary and standing orders. It includes teaching people to do the right thing and even persuading them by precept and incentive; it includes inspiring them by tradition and example.' (Barry, 1965:91). However, in the turbulent global environment of increased competition and information technology, traditional bureaucratic methods for processing information and reaching decisions, such as the use of rules and procedures, are proving increasingly inadequate. Under the Total Quality Management concept, motivation is concerned with delegating responsibility for the control of production problems and their causes to all workers in the organization under an imperative to continually improve. All the same, this is problematic, for if working conditions are deteriorating, all the rhetoric in the world about Total Quality Management may be futile.

> Unless market growth can be attained, TQM does not seem to offer a viable future prospect. This is because continuous improvement inevitably engenders job losses for both shopfloor employees and middle management. (McCabe, 1999:687)

With growth, the morale-motivation relationship is more certain.

> Southwest has learned that when employees are trusted to apply common sense and ingenuity to a problem, they come up with far better solutions than the company could have managed. They can quickly respond to customer demands and can direct their energies toward seizing market opportunities when time is critical. This demonstrates that people become

motivated, act responsibly and do more than expected when they are given freedom to think on their own. (Ohanessian & Kleiner, 1999)

 Controlling

We are discussing control here as part of the managerial process. Meanings of control can, of course, extend as far as ownership. After the sale of 49 per cent of Virgin Atlantic to Singapore Airlines, Richard Branson denied that he had been forced into the deal to ensure the survival of his airline and said that he would never surrender control of it.

> The airline is not for sale and never will be for sale. It is my baby and something I am immensely proud of. (Harrison, 1999)

However, for the most part, when we are discussing control in relation to human resource management,

> management, by definition, is concerned with tasks that require it to engage and co-ordinate the services of subordinates so that the avoidance of these tasks amounts to an abrogation of its fundamental role. If management is not accepting responsibility for the control of labour, then it is not managing. (Anthony, 1986:1)

In one aspect of the controlling activity, a manager attempts to validate plans by comparing actual performance with what was planned. If there is any deviation from plan, this should be measured in some way in order to provide criteria for future validation. Then decisions must be taken about whether to alter the business strategy or to remotivate the organization in order to close the gap between actual and planned performance. The control activity may need an accurate and rapid feedback on what is happening.

> In airlines this involves various monitoring and inspection procedures. Budget control summaries and data processing are examples of feedbacks. (Barry, 1965:91)

The available data is usually much more accurate and up to date since the installation of computerized reservation systems. This is technical control but it is only part of control that is virtually synonymous with management. Peter Anthony (1986:101), while properly insistent on managers' responsibility for the control of labour, reckons that their authority must rest on a moral base and not from a resort to 'legitimatory and and technical management theory (that) protect managers from the sceptical examination of outsiders and prevent managers from seeing themselves. Both are obstacles in the development of any theoretical exploration of management and its relationship with labour.' Managers who cling to a purely technical view of their practice,look to Organization Theory and management theory for 'objective' knowledge that will allow them, as it were, to get above and outside of their situation and manipulate others as one might manipulate objects. However, the best that Organization Theory has to offer is understanding that - though never complete - might allow us as individuals to develop forms of social relationships that are more constructive. Acknowledging the communicative character of interaction between managers and staff points to the inadequacy of purely technical versions of management control and in its place, the possibility of moral forms of social control - grounded in negotiated understanding. As Anthony puts it,

> the authority must be achieved, won, rather than imposed; it cannot be sought by coercion or by the deceptive application of psychological tricks. (1986:198)

Leadership

It has been argued that 'the personality and management style of the CEO in the airline clearly dictates the behaviour of the employees in that industry'. (Seal & Kleiner, 1999). The research contrasted chief executives of prominent airlines in the USA and 'clearly concluded that the management style of the CEO is one of the key factors that contribute to the success or failure of an airline'. In Europe also this deduction may be drawn from the resignation of Bernard Attali as president of Air France in 1992 and Robert Ayling as chairman of BA in 2000.

Not an easy concept to define,

> leadership may be considered as the process of influencing the activities of an organized group in its efforts toward goal setting and goal achievement. (Stogdill 1950:3)

Later definitions tended to perceive the leader as a 'manager of meaning'. (Smircich & Morgan, 1982). That is to say that 'leadership is seen as a process whereby the leader identifies for subordinates what is important – defining organizational reality for others'. (Bryman, 1996:279). More recently, theorizing about leadership has emphasised transformation. 'The transforming leader raises the aspirations of followers such that the leader's and the followers' aspirations are fused'. (Bryman:280). The central element of this was seen to be articulating a vision to transform followers and organizations in accordance with that vision. 'Writers on charismatic leadership also depicted vision as central to such leadership in organizational settings,' (Bryman:281) unsurprisingly, since a vision or mission is one defining characteristic of charismatic leadership. One study analysed four stages in such leadership: (i) formulating the vision; (ii) communicating the vision by denigrating the status quo and devising a rhetoric to clarify the vision; (iii) building trust in the vision; (iv) helping others achieve the vision by leading by example.

It is generally in the third and fourth stages where attempts to carry visionary leadership in corporate organizations go wrong. It could also be at the second stage where too many leaders resort to hyperbole that just does not make sense in relation to the facts of life faced by followers in their day-to-day working situation. Consider Robert Ayling's 'Leadership 2000' project:

> My vision is not only to maintain the pre-eminence of British Airways in the world airline industry but to make this company the best-managed in Britain within five years. Of course, we have to think of our customers first, second, third, fourth and last. But one of the factors that will decide our pre-eminence in the future, that will allow us to do the best by all our customers, is our management style. It must be the best there is. (Harris, 1995:25)

Instead, during his four years as chief executive, BA lost both reputation and market share; its profits evaporated and the share price was lower than when he took over. As for trust, staff morale slumped, quality of service deteriorated and Mr.Ayling was personally despised by many of his employees. The loss of trust occurred mainly during the industrial disputes of 1996 and 1997.

Similarly, Bob Crandall, CEO of American Airlines until 1998, was 'considered a relentless visionary who dazzled the industry with a series or remarkable innovations including Super Saver fares and a profitable electronic ticketing system. Under Crandall, American developed technology to distribute tickets through its Sabre system of travel agent computer terminals. It then used the data to price its tickets more judiciously, a technique known as yield management. However, when it came to dealing with people, especially those who worked for him, he was less agile.' (Seal & Kleiner). Again there is a parallel in that Crandall faced a dispute with the pilots' union – in 1997, a year after the pilots strike at BA. Crandall decreed that American's new regional jets could be flown only by lower-paid pilots from another union. The pilots did not trust him, among other reasons, because he brought many of them in at a discount during the 1980s, maligned their intelligence in the press in the first half of the 1990s, and, continued to replace their routes with propeller flights operated by low-wage commuter pilots. They expected Crandall to violate the spirit of any collective agreement that emerged from the dispute of 1997.

By contrast, more effective leadership seems to result from leaving the vision thing to the evangelists and concentrating on basics. Michael O'Leary, CEO of Ryanair, is uncomfortable philosophizing about management: 'If most chief executives cut through the PR bullshit, they'd admit they don't know where they are going. We are all flying blind. But if you've got good people and they work hard, it'll work out.' (Brown, 2000). Such brashness was absent from Herb Kelleher who was founder, president and CEO of Southwest Airlines that O'Leary had taken as his model. Kelleher led by example, believing that he had to work harder than anybody else to show his employees that he was devoted to the business. He became one of the world's most respected CEOs, 'willing to go against established thinking, yet devotedly customer-oriented and sensitive to employees' needs.' (Seal & Kleiner, 1999). He did not lack toughness:

> In 1995, Kelleher persuaded Southwest's 2,000 pilots union to accept a tough ten-year pay contract; no guaranteed increases over the first five years, only three of just 3 per cent apiece in the second five. In exchange, the pilots would get options on 1.4 million SW shares and profit-related bonuses. He preferred to talk about the types of employees Southwest tried to attract, rather than talk about himself. He emphasised the qualities he looks for are people who are unselfish, altruistic and enjoy life. The focus is on the intangibles, the spiritual qualities and not an individual's educational experience. (Seal & Kleiner, 1999)

Is it a self-fulfilling prophecy that the boss of a profitable smaller airline is seen as a more effective leader? Not necessarily – Ryanair had lost IR£20m in four years and went through four chief executives until Michael O'Leary took over and copied Southwest's formula. Seth Schofield, CEO of USAir in the 1990s when it was making losses was well regarded. He had begun as a baggage handler in 1957 and worked hard as a manager at cultivating good relations with employees, sometimes calling workers after hours to respond to letters about the company's strategy and decisions. His dictum was 'if you are honest with people and tell them the truth, more often than not they will do the right thing'. Although the unions disagreed with his focus on wage reductions, they did consider him to be a decent employer.

Another example of a successful leader with a big airline company and one that makes this analysis somewhat less ethnocentric is Cheong Choong Kong of Singapore Airlines. His claim to charisma may be that he appears in one of SIA's in-flight movie selections:

> Passengers on SIA flights can watch Cheong Choong Kong play multiple roles in *Tiger's Whip*, a locally made comedy about an American porn star who comes to Singapore to seek a cure for his lost virility. The film was universally panned and the balding bespectacled Cheong won't win any Academy awards but he need not worry. In his day job, he has received plenty of kudos for piloting SIA to its leading position as Asia's most profitable airline. (Jayasankaran, 1999:48)

New research by the consulting firm Hay/McBer, drawing on a random sample of 3,871 executives selected from a database of more than 20,000 executives worldwide, 'takes much of the mystery out of effective leadership. The research found six distinct leadership styles, each springing from different components of emotional intelligence and, perhaps most important, the research indicates that leaders with the best results so not rely on only one leadership style; they use most of them in a given week – seamlessly and in different measure – depending on the business situation'. (Goleman, 2000:78).

Contracting

The activity of contracting is that of drawing people together for a mutual undertaking. Labour-only sub-contracting in the building industry may draw together gangs of bricklayers, carpenters, electricians and plumbers to work on a housing development. Contracting includes commercial agreements such as buying and selling, agreements on the way business will be conducted and agreements among the specialist managers in large organizations.

It is possible to find examples of airlines that operate as businesses without very much, if anything, by way of organization. At the time that

WS Barry was writing on airline management, Cyprus Airways' services were provided in cooperation with British European Airways and Olympic Airways. It must be made clear that by 1994 Cyprus Airways was a complete organization with 3 BAC 1-11s, 4 Airbus A310s and 8 Airbus 320s, organising its own production of 'arrivals'. In 1966, however, the aircraft used on the Nicosia to London, Beirut, Tel Aviv and Ankara routes were Comets owned, flown and maintained by either BEA or Olympic Airways. Cyprus Airways did not have the usual airline's flying, maintenance or purchasing organizations, so it provides a helpful example.

The basic business plan of Cyprus Airways was similar to that of any other airline, i.e. to sell 'arrivals' by air. In order to achieve this plan, they assigned their traffic rights to other airlines in return for a royalty on revenues earned from the possession of these rights.

> Would Cyprus Airways still have to be regarded as an airline if the general manager had handed over the accounting to a firm of professional accountants, the marketing to a sales agency and passenger and freight handling to other agents? Would the top person sill have been able to call the business an airline if she had been sitting in an office all by herself, just dealing with a number of contractors? Would she not have turned into a travel agent?
>
> The answer is that, even by doing away with all organization, she would not have turned herself into a travel agent. Cyprus Airways would remain an airline because its intention would still be to sell arrivals. A travel agent could not have this intention because she has no arrivals to sell. A travel agent cannot choose to produce her arrivals within her own organization or by buying them in. In other words, the travel agent does not plan a process of production or a buying programme to provide so many arrivals per month and then set out to sell this number. She is merely an intermediary. Somebody comes along with a request; she enquires to see if the request can be met.
>
> Cyprus Airways, even without an organization, would still have traffic rights, without which no arrivals can be produced. They would still be able to reverse the decision to do business without an organization and buy a fleet of aircraft to run their services. (Barry,1965:92)

In the airline industry, despite computer technology – or because of it – it is a case of *plus ca change, plus c'est la meme chose* in that senior strategists now view it as realistic to have a business with very limited organization. The use of internet technology by BA, in partnership with ten other airlines, to offer customers the opportunity to book flights directly further demonstrates this.

The Significance of the Two Concepts of 'Business' and 'Organization' in Operating an Airline

In principle, then, the use of organization in doing business may be completely abandoned in favour of doing business by contracting. Business can be conducted successfully without an organization. There are two ways of running an airline, by organization and by contracting. One of the most important skills in airline general management is the ability to strike the right balance between the alternative methods.

Until quite recently it was reasonable to accept that there were in-built tendencies for airlines to become more and more self-contained, to move from business to organization via vertical integration of activities. Freight forwarders are usually contracting agents, though some have vertically integrated forward to operating their own aircraft. Air Europe moved from being essentially a travel business to containing many elements of airline organization. Unfortunately, it was over-extended and collapsed with the recession in air travel in 1991. Dan-Air, formed in 1953 by the London family-owned shipbroker, Davies & Newman, also developed a charter business but this proved unreliable and contained the seeds of its ultimate demise in 1992.

Globalization implies more self-containment and diversification of airline businesses. However, it is also quite compatible with the prevailing business philosophy that urges the stripping-out of all activities that are not essential to the core business activity of an enterprise. Global aircraft leasing companies, such as Guinness Peat Aviation, permit airline companies to decide to lease, rather than purchase aircraft (see Chapter 9). Airline companies may sub-contract part of cleaning and catering activities. CRS may have gained more control over marketing for airline companies but they still frequently contract marketing activities to travel agents. International regulatory bodies may in the future require airlines to seek or relinquish control of CRS in the interests of competition, but this seems out of line with the form that deregulation has so far taken.

The main areas of contracting by airlines are:

(i) Manufacture of capital equipment, such as aircraft and communications equipment;

(ii) Maintenance of equipment, such as overhaul and repair of aircraft. This can create difficulties if the maintenance facilities of a rival airline have been relied upon and competition intensifies. Virgin Atlantic bought maintenance from BA at Heathrow and was faced with sharply rising costs after relations between the airlines deteroriated in 1991. Virgin switched to maintenance contract with Team, the maintenance arm of Air Lingus but that also proved unsatisfactory when deteriorating employee relations in opposition to job cuts led to individual action that disrupted maintenance scheduler.

(iii)   Temporary additions to equipment, aircraft leasing;
(iv)   Temporary additions to staff by chartering aircraft inclusive of crews;
(v)   Processing by contracting out cargo handling and use of freight forwarders;
(vi)   Marketing through travel agents, as discussed in the previous chapter.

In the turbulent environment that beset airlines in the 1990s, increased sub-contracting of peripheral activities was one change in organizational structure that may be an optional part of a strategy for change. The next chapter will examine the factors that influence the strategic decisions that managers make between the alternatives of doing work within the airline organization or putting it out to contractors.

6 Elements of Airline Organization

In the previous chapter a theory of airline organization was proposed. It is now necessary to consider the factors that influence the choices that airline managers make between the alternatives of doing work within airline organization or putting it out to contractors.

Factors Influencing Decisions on the Alternatives of Adding to Organization or Contracting

The main factors are:

(i)   Costs
(ii)   Attitudes to organization and contracting
(iii) Availability of capital
(iv)   Availability of good managers
(v)   Availability of employees, equipment and raw materials
(vi)   The concept of optimal organization
(vii) The relation between size of an airline business and its organization.

Costs

Much of the discussion about human resource management during the last 20 years cannot avoid cost reductions and job losses. In 1991, for example, Windle attempted to measure the productivity and unit costs of 27 non-US. and 14 US airlines in order to document differences. He used results from a cost function analysis to decompose productivity and unit cost differentials to determine what factors are most influential in shaping these differences and thus what forms of deregulation and rationalization are likely to increase productivity.

Rationalization does not necessarily mean cutting back your business - it should mean essentially cutting back your costs. Some operating costs are outside the control of airline managements. Rigas Doganis (1991), formerly an executive with Olympic Airways and a keen student of the airline industry, has usefully suggested three broad categories affecting costs, according to the degree that they can be influenced by management:

(i)   External economic factors over which airlines have little control. Such factors include the fuel prices and airport, en route and navigation charges. An airline has to accept these as more or less given and can only marginally mitigate their impact through negotiations with fuel suppliers and buying and selling forward. Similarly, some arrangements can be made to offset currency movements but a high rate of exchange in the airline's home country can be a serious competitive disadvantage, as shown by the SIA/Cathay Pacific contrast in chapter 8.

(ii) Two big determinants of costs over which airlines have somewhat more but still limited control are type of aircraft and the pattern of operations for which aircraft are used. Whilst there is some room for changing management strategy, the scope for change is limited by decisions taken in the past. For example, the geographical location of an airline's national home base. Note, however that Doganis does mean by this the airline's national home base; an airline can still switch its head office location, as Air France did in moving from Montparnasse in central Paris to Charles de Gaulle airport in the hopes of moving closer to the market and the point of production and symbolising organisational change. Another example is the limit imposed by bilateral air services agreements signed by national governments. It may be commented that, in this respect, the airline itself may lobby the government to be tough and restrictive, as BA did before British government negotiations with the USA air transport authorities – especially after the proposed alliance with American collapsed. Finally, for example, traffic density on its routes will limit management control over costs. Especially if there is one national flag carrier, management may not have a free hand. The pressure of the French government to reach an accommodation with the unions that led to the resignation of Bernard Attali as Air France president may be cited.

(iii) Management can be said to have complete control of marketing, product planning and financial policy. These will be discussed in later chapters in respect of their implications for human resource management. Whilst stating that most operating costs are outside the control of airline managements, Doganis does appreciate that personnel costs can be adjusted, mainly by means of raising productivity. However, there are limits here. Does the preoccupation with Total Quality Management in service industries reflect anxieties that reducing numbers employed must reduce customer service ?

Attitudes to Organization and Contracting

Prominent among strategies used by management to cut costs has been the use of sub-contracting and out-sourcing of activities that may have been traditionally carried out by airline personnel. Whether companies can take advantage of reduced market costs and derive a better performance from contractors in the market is questionable, yet highly pertinent.

> Since the externalisation of non-strategic services through outsourcing occurs in certain segments of the travel industry, it appears to fit, at least partly, the mold of post-Fordist practices. Outsourcing of ancillary activities provides numerous advantages, including the generation of external economies. Companies accrue considerable savings by buying cheaper services (e.g. aircraft maintenance or aircraft leasing) from outside specialist firms because the latter can generate scale economies. (Ioannides & Debbage, 1997:237)

The first requirement of such a programme is to decide just what are the core activities of the company and the services needed to support them. This may be done by an assessment of all departments, asking the question 'what does the department do?' Can its tasks be done more effectively outside the airline company? Each division or department must be made to justify its operation to survive. If it cannot justify its existence, then the job will be done outside the company.

We are just emerging from an era when it was not unusual for large airline companies to have their own departments covering diverse activities. For example, until quite recently, it was considered a good idea to vertically integrate airlines into the hotel business, with the aim of offering an all-encompassing service to the customer. However, United and JAL found that such activities were peripheral and not germane to the main business. It was an unfruitful form of expansion and was stopped. Because they are ancillary operations, management cannot be expert in the techniques involved, especially the control of human resources. Consequently, the divisions cannot be authentic profit centres and tend to become flabby. Because they are not part of the mainstream operations, they may not receive the necessary funding to keep up their productivity. Indeed, when there are cash flow difficulties, these divisions are vulnerable. It may, therefore, be more logical to sell them. Air France was compelled to sell its Meridien hotels division but commercial logic also dictated such a move when the mainstream business was losing millions. Similarly, Aer Lingus was forced to seek a buyer for its Copthorne hotels division.

There was a time when such vertical integration made economic sense as a defence against opportunistic re-contracting by independent firms or in order to internalise management control over input quality or even in pursuit of monopolization. In the much more intensely competitive environment of the last 20 years, such logic has been turned upside down.

The main sorts of sub-contracting by airline companies may be summarized as:

(i)   Manufacture of capital equipment, such as offices, hangars, workshop, aircraft and communications gear;
(ii) Processing of raw materials and data, such as carriage by other operators, passenger and freight handling (freight forwarders offer a service that would be 'off-line' for airline companies);
(iii) Maintenance of buildings and the maintenance, overhaul and repair of aircraft;
(iv) Marketing through travel agents;
(v)   Temporary additions to operating fleet strength, such as by chartering aircraft and crews;
(vi) Temporary additions to equipment, such as bare-hull aircraft chartering.

Some companies lease aircraft on a long term basis, finding that this gives them more flexibility over costs. Aircraft leasing is discussed in Chapter 9.

Contracting is never self-evidently a cheaper or better option than in-house operation. For one thing, it necessitates exceptionally vigilant accounting practice. In 1993 BA acknowledged that police had been investigating a possible fraud in its Heathrow property maintenance division. The fraud was alleged to involve payments made by BA to property sub-contractors for maintenance work that was never done. Some managers were believed to have colluded with the contractors, in return for benefits, such as holidays. It was reported that up to a dozen people, including BA employees, were arrested in connection with the fraud.

Availability of Capital

Not so many years ago, availability of capital would not have been considered problematic. It encouraged extensive organisational structure among airlines. Among higher income per head countries, apart from the USA, national airlines were either publicly owned or strongly influenced managerially by national governments. They may have been obliged to raise finance capital at commercial rates of interest and meet commercial criteria but their profitability would not enter too strongly into calculations. Indeed, low rates of return might be justified by the public service nature of some airline activities.

As discussed earlier, the trouble with this is that the cost of running parts of airlines additional services were not easily isolated. Their effect was obscure and it became difficult for shareholder, government and management to judge the efficiency of the commercial core of the airline. This would have been the case with the Philippine Airlines' example discussed in chapter 2.

> In France in the late 1970s, the development of domestic air routes, mainly served by the state-owned Air Inter (now part of Air France), was considered to be a contribute to the spatial planning and development of France. The result was a veritable airline mania: every town of any claim to importance wanted to have its own air links so that it would not be isolated and so that it would be in a position to attract the industrial territory developments that would create employment. The setting up of these lines and the responsibility for their deficits were the province of the town councils and the chambers of commerce, assisted from 1972 by subsidies form DATAR, the government organization for strategic spatial planning. Services to towns not served by Air Inter were provided by regional companies, the so-called third-level carriers. The network was developed in a random manner, without any serious study of the market. (Pinchemel, 1987)

Publicly owned or publicly subsidised airlines and their employees tend to become clients of the state. In the more deflationary, high interest rate climate of the last 20 years, governments wanted to roll back this commitment to their purse strings. Airline managements too could see the advantages of commercial freedom, not least in managing employees. Japan Airlines and BA were privatized in the mid 1980s.

The latest European airlines to break away from state control were Lufthansa in 1994 and Iberia in 1999. Prerequisites for Lufthansa were cost-cutting and productivity gains that led Paribas Capital Markets to predict pre-tax profits of over DM200 million for 1994 and a negotiated solution to the complex problem of the state-run employee pension scheme. According to the executive chair, Jürgen Weber, 'many people thought it was not possible to solve the pension fund issue and that we would never get Lufthansa out of the red. Unions and management can take pride that they worked together to achieve these supposedly impossible goals'. (Walters, 1994).

Consequently, Weber found common cause with BA and KLM in opposing state subsidies to rivals, such as Air France. Although, as a member of the European Commission sub-committee to examine the industry, he had helped to write the report that supported 'one time, last time' aid to help ailing airlines restructure, Weber reckoned that 'the money for Air France was too high - it would cover our total group debt'. (Walters, 1994).

Availability of Good Managers

The theory of how availability of good managers can affect organizational behaviour has been developed by Oliver Williamson (1975). His hypothesis was that the employment relation allowed long run incentives of a promotion ladder sort to be effectuated that are unavailable in market contracting. He qualified this by saying that firms have limitations when it comes to the award of large bonus payments. First, such payments may be regarded as a status threat by higher-level managers. Second, awarding bonuses for exceptional performance introduces transactions-specific elements into the contract. This imperils the integrity of the employment relation because the long term systems considerations on which it relies would give way to a series of *quid pro quo* bargains. Given that the relation between the parties is commonly of a small numbers sort, on account of task idiosyncrasies, transaction costs would quickly escalate as the pay system became expensive to administer. Any organisational imperative to maintain strict correspondence between income and hierarchy naturally serves as a disincentive to entrepreneurial types who might otherwise be prepared to accept a position in the company.

Such logic has been thoroughly subverted by the economic and technological changes since Williamson produced this hypothesis. On the supply side, performance-related pay and the injection of market relations into the organisation has undermined equity and long term service arguments (though their displacement does not prove that they were wrong). On the demand side, flatter management structures and wholesale job cuts have reduced the demand for managers.

Availability of Operatives, Equipment and Raw Materials

The expansion of individual airline companies can be impeded in the short term by shortages in particular categories of employees. It could be, for instance, that there are insufficient trained pilots. Doganis has quoted the case of Singapore Airlines, as a result of rapid expansion, having to employ many expatriate pilots during the 1980s, thereby raising its average pay for pilots to levels high relative to neighbouring airlines. In the long run, its aviation culture has developed and now most pilots are Singaporean. During the UK recession of the early 1990s, Cathay Pacific was able to hire many partly but not fully trained BA pilots on the short term contracts that could be treated as a component of the full training programme.

Availability is the main reason why airline companies are reluctant to fully contract out the vital activities of catering and maintenance. Instead, these are usually carried out by a wholly-owned subsidiary or by a jointly owned firm. BA had such an arrangement with Forte until the latter's takeover by Granada. In general, 'airlines rely heavily on contract caterers. The worldwide in-flight catering market grossed $9 billion in 1993, led by LSG Lufthansa Service/SKYCHEFS which served 310,000 meals daily to over 200 carriers at 72 different locations. LSG, which employed over 18,000 workers, earned $1.34 billion, representing a 15 per cent market share. Indeed, the top four airline caterers worldwide controlled half the market.' (Ioannides & Debbage, 1997:237). Korean Air was a monopoly supplier of catering services to airlines in South Korea. Faced with competition from a new rival, Asiana (formed in 1988), Korean Air increased its prices for catering, forcing Asiana to form its own catering arm with Scandinavian Air Services.

In the European Union, the Acquired Rights Directive (77/187) does make a difference to management decisions to sub-contract activities already done in-house. Aer Lingus was negotiating in 1997 with several prospective companies interested in acquiring a majority stake in its aircraft maintenance subsidiary, TEAM Aer Lingus. Before any sale, the Aer Lingus Group first had to negotiate a collective agreement with the unions to compensate 1,200 of TEAM's 1,500 employees for agreeing voluntarily to relinquish their legal rights to remain as group employees. They had gained these guarantees in the form of 'letters of comfort' when they transferred from the former maintenance and engineering division to work for the newly created subsidiary, TEAM, in 1990. Aer Lingus did not deny press speculation that the compensation would be somewhere between IEP5,000 and IEP20,000, depending on service, for each worker. It was also noted that any resolution of the conflict would require more than an industrial relations agreement as any deal entered into voluntarily could be challenged in the law courts by those who held the original guarantees. Observers agreed that only a legal agreement could replace the original letters of comfort and would take a collective and individual form. (Sheehan & Geary, 1997).

For these reasons, national flag carrier airlines have to be more circumspect about the widespread tendency to sub-contract and out-source peripheral activities. Long before the flexible firm was even debated as a viable or coherent strategy, Chandler (1986:71) found that 'sub-contracting was double-edged; on the one hand, it was a means by which some managements shuffled off their responsibility but at the same time it could be used to reassert managerial control and prerogatives by proxy'. Even for smaller airlines, such a rationale for sub-contracting does not exist to the same extent as in manufacturing. However,it can be done and is known as 'wet leasing'. In February 1995, as part of its restructuring battle with the pilots' union, Alitalia announced that crews and planes would be leased from Ansett, the Australian company. Aiming to cut costs, the management had signed a renewable six-month rental contract fot two Boeing 767-300 ERs, including crews, from Ansett. The Italian pilots' union protested that Alitalia was turning itself into a kind of travel agency and announced a series of strikes.

The hiring of whole aircraft to carry passengers or freight can take various forms. There are 'journey' charters in which aircraft and their crews are hired to undertake particular journeys to particular places at particular times. Leasing complete flights is always simpler than expanding your own capacity and can be realised at acceptable cost levels, as was the intention in the Alitalia case. Secondly, there are 'period' charters where aircraft and crews are hired by the week or month on a dry lease (without fuel) for unspecified journeys. Thirdly, there are 'bare-hull charters in which the aircraft is hired without crew and usually without fuel. 'Wet leasing' was an issue in the contentious negotiations between the UK and USA over a revised air services agreement; American cargo airlines already had the right to lease their aircraft and crews within the EU but 'Fly America' policy, rules on foreign investment and wet leasing of aircraft rankled with the British cargo airlines and BA.

Apart from aircraft leasing and chartering, the main area for sub-contracting by airlines is data processing. Data processing employees may be not be so much sub-contracted as employed at a distance. In 1983 American Airlines sacked 200 employees at its data processing office in Tulsa, Oklahoma and moved the work to Barbados. By 1990 American employed more than a thousand data processors in Barbados and the Dominican Republic to enter names and flight numbers from used airline tickets. The tickets were flown in daily, processed and the data sent by satellite to a computer information bank in Dallas. BA has used distancing to employ somewhat more skilled staff. It set up its curiously named Message Editing Unit in New Delhi in 1990, attracted by the availability of university graduates with the necessary computing skills and the low wage and overhead costs. Working in shifts, the unit could decipher and rectify corrupted and inaccurate messages from 20 computer reservation systems around the world on which BA flights were booked.

The Concept of the Optimal Organization

An organization of optimal size, working at full capacity, would have lowest average costs per unit of production, taking into account all costs of production. The concept is applicable to the whole organization and its elements. If total organization is at optimal size, an increase or decrease in any one part of it will increase total costs per unit of production. However, a complete organization that is at optimal size may contain elements, none of which are at optimal size. In other words, the optimal size of total organization may be attained by a compromise in which the size of each element diverges from its optimum - in order to fit with the other elements. In studies of Japanese human resource management, the importance of organizational 'fit' is often emphasised (Oliver and Wilkinson).   One adjustment that can be made by passenger airlines is by cargo handling in wide-bodied aircraft. The amount of space left over in the cargo hatch after passengers' baggage is loaded allows airlines to act as freight carriers without buying specialist aircraft. In 1985 Al Hicks, vice-president of specialist air cargo carrier Flying Tiger (acquired by Federal Express in 1988), remarked that passenger airlines 'only view cargo as an additional revenue service - something in their empty bellies is better than nothing'. Regarding the lowness of the rates quoted by passenger carriers to the USA, he questioned whether the airlines offering them could really be concerned about what their real costs were in handling this freight. (Eaton,1994).

It might be thought that passenger aircraft are best for shippers because they are free, frequent and fast. That is, space for freight is available on passenger aircraft whether it is used or not and can therefore be regarded as being produced at cost. Therefore, carriers are able to fix low rates. Passenger services are are more frequent than all cargo services and finally, faster aircraft are used for passenger services. However, timings for passenger services are not necessarily best for freight. Freight holds in passenger aircraft must be smaller, restricting size and variety of goods that can be carried. The best embarkation points for passengers may not be the best loading points for cargo and outward and return passenger services are unlikely to be the ideal pattern for freight service.

Paradoxically, amidst a general tendency to sub-contracting, a traditional area of sub-contracting may be brought inside larger airlines, as a result of new technology. Travel agents essentially supply a selling service to airlines. To the airlines, this is part of their marketing management, through CRS. However, to the travel agents, the job of selling airline tickets is their production: their marketing arrangements are about selling their services as go-betweens (intermediaries) to both airlines and travelling customers. Agents' production expenses consist of office rents, sales representatives' salaries etc. Agents' revenue is derived from their principals - the airlines - though they are the custodians of the cash from travellers, earning for their services, a fixed percentage of money collected on behalf of the principals. For CRS service, sometimes travel agents are charged a small sign-up fee but the bulk of CRS revenue accrues from participating airlines who pay for each fare segment booked. The policy of airlines has been to sub-contract a great deal to travel agents in order to concentrate on core activities. However, the CRSs have acted as learning organizations to teach airlines about yield management and how much revenue they are missing from sub-contracting and paying commission to travel agents. In February 2000, BA announced a £100m strategy to increase its internet presence, including an online travel agency to be owned jointly by most of the major European airlines. The company had already announced a new payment structure for travel agents, eliminating commission. BA wanted 'its new payment structure to reflect the growing use of direct-line payment for tickets under which consumers get them over the telephone or internet from the airline, cutting out the agent. Sales through agents are unlikely to disappear but will increasingly be reserved for consumers needing special advice or discounts.' (Marsh,

2000). One problem with such innovations is that the potential for fraud using the internet and electronic ticketless booking systems is limitless.

The Relation Between the Size of an Airline Business and its Organization

It remains true, to generalize, that the limits of airline organization are determined by the size of its business.   Size of business is largely determined by the demand for arrivals of passengers and freight by air and - marginally - by the demand for additional services, such as doing maintenance work for other airlines. The limits are, therefore, not static but grow and contract roughly with the size of the market.

In principle, an airline organization may grow to the size at which its rate of production can maximise the profit to be obtained by organization. Both organization and contractual activities may bring profits to an airline and each should be fixed at a level to bring maximum profit.

However, as Giovanni Bisignani of Alitalia has pointed out (Simonian, 1992), 'people used to think that airlines could overcome efficiency problems simply by growing. That is no longer possible. The market is not expanding as before and yields are falling. The only way to drive down costs in a market that has become more volatile is to be flexible. The danger is that greater size leads to less flexibility.'

In assessing actual capacity and costs in order to decide whether an operation can be subtained or not, the amortization rate and unit costs must be assessed conservatively and parsimoniously.   In her classic but neglected study, Margaret Chandler (1964) provided a framework for analysing the decision to sub-contract:

'In developing a model for the contracting-out decision, one might very well have accomplished little more than the precise pinning down of imprecise data. However, our approach was not normative and we did not have the goal of reforming managerial thought processes.   Rather, we wanted to treat the decision as an organizational process – to study the flow of events and changes in the process over time. Our model was based on the conviction that there was, after all, some rigour in the process and that, to a certain extent, it was dominated by a limited number of objective and measurable factors.' (Chandler, 1964:259).

Chandler's book is difficult to come by these days. So it may be useful to summarize its main features, modifying it to apply to airline organization. The initial stages involve the simple determination of the main units of analysis and of the relationships among them. The salient units include members of 'inside' and 'outside' forces. These would include the unions for ground staff, cabin crews and pilots, and, for some airlines, maintenance workers. Outside forces are contractors. Other units would be human resources/personnel and operations management. Members of these groups are both decision-makers and representatives of special interests. Operations management will have a bigger initial decision function than human resources. Apart from handling worker complaints about contracting out, HRM will rarely have active decision-making powers in this area.

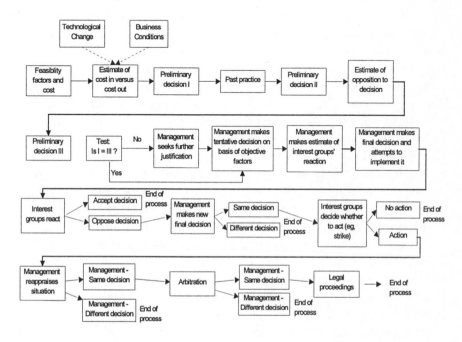

Flowchart: the Contracting-out decision

The flow chart summarizes the crucial steps in the decision process. Data about factors such as the availability of contractors and the costs of labour and materials are the basis of making an estimate of the relative costs of the two alternatives. They are made in the light of environmental factors, such as business conditions and the rate of technological change. Preliminary Decision I is reached and the process may possibly end now.

However, the decision may be altered by evaluation of Decision I in the light of past practice that may lead to Preliminary Decision II. An estimate of the potential opposition to the proposed action may lead to Preliminary Decision III. At this point, it may be that consideration of past practice and an estimate of opposition to the decision cause a change in direction of the decision.   If the two decisions are different, the management faces a dilemma and must attempt to resolve it by seeking further justification for its action. Having completed this step, management makes another tentative decision and also makes a new estimate of the interest groups' reaction to the decision. This step may include consultation with them.

The interest groups are faced with a definite decision and they react to it. When all the interest groups have reacted to the decision, the process may end with all of them accepting it. However, groups able to mobilize pressure may oppose the decision and take steps to demonstrate their displeasure. Management, in turn, will react to their demonstration and make a new final decision. The new final decision may also be a simple repetition of the original one, perhaps with new terminology. Having received a counter-challenge, the interest groups will then consider a future course of action. They may simply drop the matter or decide to trade their grievances for other concessions (see the following chapter). In either instance, the process may have reached its end point and management may proceed with its original decision.

However, if pressure-generating factors are strong, the interest groups may take further action. The inside (intra-organizational) workers, through their unions, are most capable of a persistent challenge. In the face of pressures, such as strike action, management will again appraise the situation. If the managers do not make acceptable concessions, the door is open for a third party. In some countries, the inside union is much better able to extend the process beyond the point of management's final refusal. It may take the matter to arbitration or may resort to legal proceedings, as in the Aer Lingus TEAM decision.

Chandler pointed out that this model was limited to the flow of events surrounding a particular decision. The nature of the decision model was to be interpreted 'not as a denial of the significance of the manager as a decision-maker but rather as a recognition of the fact that, in the case of the contracting-out decision, the core of the process often lay in the interactions of the pressure or interest groups inside and outside the firm'.

In conclusion, the relation between the size of an airline's 'business' and its 'organization' is not a simple one. Airline organizations do not always grow at the same pace as the businesses themselves. The maximum size of organization for any given size of business will depend on the relative costs of contracting and organization. The nature of competition among airlines means that contracting can have a higher actual cost in the long run than might be the case in other industries. The rationality of control by economic market forces explains only in part the coverage of, for instance, maintenance outsourcing.

Even among medium-sized airline companies, effective management control can design organization with little in the way of contracting. Martin Air Holland, the third biggest independent non-scheduled airline in the world and the most successful in Europe, exemplifies the way that management is about control. The company decided on a devolved corporate structure and consequently thrived when many bigger airlines were struggling, making a profit of nearly £15 million in 1993.

At monthly meetings, everyone received a copy of each other's monthly reports in an effort to avoid the 'civil service syndrome' that company president Martin Schroder reckoned to be endemic in excessively compartmentalised multinationals. However, devolution of authority did not mean that the president lost sight of issues once they had left the boardroom. Control over the 'administrative tendency' was a key element of the corporate philosophy since MAC's humble beginnings in 1958 with a staff of four conducting sight seeing flights over Amsterdam in a De Havilland Dove carrying nine passengers. In 1966 the company became Martin Air Holland and in 1994 employed 2,100.

Controlling market segments to achieve, a 50:50 ratio between passengers and cargo was central to Martin Air's strategy. 'The key lies in segmenting the market to spread risks as evenly as possible over four markets, making us less dependent on fluctuations in individual segments', stated Martin Schroder. (Spinks, 1994). Martinair's subsidiaries complemented its aviation activities, while providing diversification. Martinair Party Service organises lunches, dinners and receptions and is the biggest service of the kind in the Netherlands. Marfo produced frozen meals for airlines and other organisations. Martinair Promotions, a multi-service bureau, conducted product promotions and exhibitions at shopping centres, on beaches and in the air. Cost control, over airline activities in the four main market segments and over the three subsidiaries was integral to strategy. A special committee of four executives examined all spending proposals and exercised restraint over them.

PART III
INDUSTRIAL RELATIONS
AND HUMAN RESOURCE
MANAGEMENT

7 Industrial Relations

As in other aspects of business management, there has been a vigorous debate between those who believe that fundamental changes have occurred in the managerial approach to industrial relations over the last decade and those who persist in the view that, beneath the cyclical downturn, the essential procedural relationship of management and employees remains much the same. In the first view, the rise of globalization and the power of the multinational company has been instrumental in promoting a human resource management approach that is strategic but does not involve industrial relations *per se*. Those who envisage management-employee relations as a pendulum may perceive the present period of industrial relations - a period characterized by subdued union bargaining power - as similar to what occurred in previous deflationary eras. They see current bargaining outcomes as nothing new and imply that they will be reversed if and when employment conditions recover.

Some credence must be given to the second point of view in that, semantically, it is a truism. So long as a functional area or subject of study using the nomenclature 'industrial relations' exists, it must be about the socio-economic transaction between employer or manager and employees. Industrial relations is about the rules governing employment and the relations between managers and employees in determining thise rules. The character of such relations will vary from differences to disputes and to agreements. Industrial Relations will always 'refer to the manner in which the issues between employers and employees are resolved, in terms of negotiation, consultation, mediation, conciliation and arbitration' (Barry:158) and there will always be forms of conflict, even if suppressed.

What has changed is the nature of the organizations that employers and employees have created to handle these relations. Until quite recently, the industrial relations branches of airline personnel departments and workers' associations at shop floor level were often joined to the big employers' federations and trade unions respectively. Each of these would then work through the voluntary or state organs of conciliation or arbitration. However, decentralization of such negotiation arrangements has occurred. The employers are the prime movers here, with the unions largely unable to do other than react.

With few exceptions, airline companies have opted for enterprise autonomy in their industrial relations, detaching themselves from employers' federations. On the common industrial relations issues, such as pay and hours of work, managers seek to exert cost control by relating them to productivity at company or workplace levels. Unions have had little option but to hang on doggedly, supporting their members in what Professor William Brown (1985) called *de facto* enterprise unionism at the workplace level. For one of the burning issues of the industry has not changed, except quantitatively, having become much deeper with profound effects: The industry's economic ups and downs have undermined the security of employment of large numbers. Recession, aggravated by deregulation, has revealed high over-capacity in the industry with resultant problems for employers in handling retrenchment, redundancy or, euphemistically, 'early retirement'. This was one of the methods that Air France attempted in the strategic plan, CAP 93.

As in other industries, the changes in industrial relations practices and procedures have mainly emanated from structural and technological change. Deregulation, inaugurated in the USA in 1978 but spreading to Europe by the 1990s, intensified competition as its proponents intended, at least in the short term. The superimposition of recession after the Gulf war obliged airlines to retrench as they were incurring huge losses. Employees were on the receiving end of all this, notably at BA where senior management had already had a battle with the ground staff unions and later made 22,000 job cuts in readiness for privatization. It has to be said that it was largely as a result of this tight cost control (and some postponement of fleet replacement) that BA was one of few western airlines showing a profit from 1991-93.

Other European, American and Australian airlines were obliged to follow suit, adopting new technology and hub and spoke systems to rationalize and acquire economies of scale. However, the main objective of various strategic plans, adopted by airlines, such as Air France, was flexibility, particularly numerical flexibility. 'Strategy' may actually be the key word that is the leitmotiv of the fundamental change that has occurred in the conduct of industrial relations in that industrial relations is 'guilty by association'. Strategists make bureaucracy a scapegoat for previous errors and industrial relations procedures are depicted as part of the bureaucracy. Of course it remains true that, as Barry put it, the managements of most of the world's major airlines are involved with industrial relations. He added that most of them have permanent 'machinery' for dealing with workers' demands for increased pay and better working conditions. In the last decade the inverted commas would be better placed around the word 'permanent', for the machinery has been considerably rejigged.

Whilst it remains necessary for most of them to have procedures for dealing with disputes between employers and employees, the fundamental procedural norm has shifted towards the managerial prerogative. 'Constitutions and rules of procedure differ from airline to airline. The number and nature of industrial relations institutions vary widely. The degree of autonomy of the machinery differs.' (Barry:159). It is, however, the common constitutional principles that have altered throughout the industry and what can be more fundamental than constitutional change?

> Constitutions usually attempt to embody, in a single or small number of documents, fundamental activities and institutions. Constitutions are not always wholly or even partly written. Conventions established by the spoken word and custom and usage can sometimes work as effectively as a written constitution. De Toqueville, in his "La Democratie en Amerique", refers to a constitution as 'an instrument of special sanctity, distinct in character from all other laws and alterable only by a peculiar process. This is true of constitutions of industrial relations. They are difficult to alter. (Barry:161)

A crucial constitutional issue is union recognition. Under strategic human resource management, companies have approached this in two ways. The usual is to continue recognition but to gradually attempt to sideline the unions by supplanting their functions. In an era of cost competition and worries about wage costs, this demands considerable ingenuity. The rationale for smaller new entrant airlines is that they may avoid the presumed additional costs associated with collective bargaining. Hence the alternative approach is outright avoidance of union recognition.

Air France and BA: A Comparative Approach

It can be demonstrated that airline managers throughout Europe have been 'following the leader' in introducing new management approaches (Warhurst, 1996:259) and that these approaches amount to a constitutional change in the management of industrial relations towards an HRM approach. In theory, 'strategic HRM takes a long-term perspective and is concerned with issues such as corporate culture and individual career development, as well as the availability of people with the right skills. It incorporates redundancy and recruitment planning and is increasingly focused on the concept of the flexible workforce.' (Price, 1997:156).

Yet, strategy has different meanings. The usually understood meaning is 'strategy as planning'; by a highly rational decision-making process, choices are made from among future options and these decisions are the implemented by managers. At least one alternative perspective on strategy is, however, possible. That is that strategy need not be deliberate but can emerge incrementally. We could therefore distinguish between what might be called *paradigmatic* strategic change industrial relations and HRM, meaning a fundamental and possibly revolutionary change in the constitution of industrial relations, and, incremental strategic change that only gradually emerges and incrementally alters industrial relations procedures. To do so, we compare recent HRM strategy at BA and Air France. They are fierce commercial rivals, directly competing on many routes. There have already been constitutional changes affecting management at both, particularly BA since its privatization. The difference is that BA has attempted to adopt a paradigmatic strategy, while Air France was forced to pursue incremental strategy.

Soon after Robert Ayling took over as chief executive in January 1996, he announced a 'Step Change' strategy, believing that BA still had some of the trappings of the nationalized industry and that it was not as efficient or competitive as it might be. Despite the appellation of the strategy, however, it was paradigmatic change that he had in mind because it entailed a strong attack on the unions by means of pay cuts and sub-contracting. The over-riding aim was to deliver £1 billion of cost savings by the year 2000 - a paradigmatic strategy and one that fitted well with BA's aim to become a global airline company, perhaps, but also a high-risk strategy.

All looked well in 1996 as BA celebrated 10 years as a private company by reporting a 9.2 per cent rise in profits to £583 million for the first three quarters of 1996. This compared with Air France's £372 million loss. The BA profits could also permit bonuses to staff and for those opting to use some or all of their bonus to acquire shares through BA's profit-sharing scheme, a corporate identity revamp was begun. Unfortunately, from this promising beginning there grew a series of strategic mistakes that led to criticism of the senior management by financial institutions for not being conciliatory in industrial relations.

First, BA managed to provoke its pilots into voting 90 per cent in favour of strike action on a 94 per cent turnout. Although, the pilots had benefitted from the bonus system, they rejected a proposed 3.6 per cent increase, were disgruntled at being excluded from an improvement to pensions and suspicious about the long-term dilution effects of pay cuts for newly recruited pilots. Their union, BALPA, suspected an ulterior management motive to undermine its bargaining relationship. Robert Ayling was a staunch advocate of profit-sharing and talking directly to staff, thereby circumventing the unions who apparently had no place in the airline business.

Eventually the dispute was resolved with the help of an outside consultant. BA and BALPA agreed 10 'guiding principles' designed to create a 'new relationship imbued with open-ness, confidentiality and mutual understanding of each other's objectives'. (Barrie, 1997). This was it - Human Resource Management as defined by mutuality (Walton, 1985) at least - but it had taken a threatened strike to achieve it.

Furthermore, there was no sign of mutuality elsewhere. According to Walton, mutuality entailed commitment and commitment could not logically exist alongside plans to sub-contract part of the organization that must necessarily result in less favourable terms and conditions of employment. That might be necessary, indeed inescapable, as part of the £1 billion business efficiency program but one would have to be rather crass to perceive the logic of cost-savings as not meaning cuts in pay or numbers employed or both. Sub-contractors may be more efficient although this is far from certain - and there is a presumed reason. Hence BA seemed prepared to contract out engineering, baggage handling and check-in work - some 5000 job cuts in 18 months. BA Engineering had been restructured as an autonomous business and BA had not ruled out allowing private investors to take stakes in it. Catering was definitely being sub-contracted.

Sub-contracting is a salient issue in industrial relations. Although it is topical on account of the emphasis on flexible production and vertical disintegration, (Ioannides & Babbage,1997:229) it is far from new. Margaret Chandler researched it in what is now a neglected classic: *Management Rights and the Union Interest* (1962). She found that 'sub-contracting was double-edged: on the one hand, it was a means by which some managements shuffled off their responsibilities but, at the same time, it could be used to reassert managerial control and prerogatives by proxy. Sub-contracting offered an escape from the rebarbative and time-consuming obligations of the employment relationship itself'. (Aldridge, 1976:79). The union interests are obvious: sub-contracting may mean job losses and almost certainly does mean less likelihood of union recognition for bargaining purposes from the sub-contractor. In this case, the TGWU saw the contracting out of catering services as part of a move to de-recognize unions at Heathrow and other airports, although management dismissed this as nonsense. (Harper, 1997). The phases of the dispute may be seen to correspond with the flow-chart on sub-contracting decisions in the previous chapter.

The main 'inside' resistance to economies that contributed to the business efficiency programme came from cabin crew. BA had made a pay offer, accepted by the breakaway union, Cabin Crew '89, with 3000 members. BASSA, the restored cabin crew branch of the TGWU, claimed that the pay offer really concealed a 19 per cent pay cut for new recruits, while apparent rises for present staff were to be achieved by consolidating overtime and allowances. In one example, a steward's basic pay increased by £116 a month but on his first 6 day trip to Kuala Lumpur he lost £148 in overtime pay and £12.60 mileage allowance for travel to work in unsocial hours. His reaction may be viewed as typical of 'insider' workers when faced with the threat of a two tier pay structure where new recruits are paid substantially less than existing staff: 'They are bringing in recruits on £8000 a year and what's that going to do to our pay in the future?' (Milne, 1997).

Consequently, the TGWU members voted 3-1 in favour of strike action, 6400 for and 1770 against. Robert Ayling's reaction seemed to convey the real perceptions of management about the union: 'There is no reason or justification for this strike. We will not be held back by 1970s trade unionism. Even if it comes to a strike, we will put our customers first.' As last ditch negotiations broke down, he added that the union had no interest in the competitiveness of the business and did not recognize the need for change in modern industrial relations. It was BA management that appeared confrontational as communications director announced that management had decided to use what it believed was a procedural flaw in the strike ballot to 'recover from the union some of the losses incurred' with the human resources director claiming that 'there is an important principle at stake. This is an unlawful strike.' (Milne & MacAskill, 1997).

The strike began at the worst possible time, in July at the start of the holiday season, amidst recriminations about the alleged cost of the corporate identity revamp and union ripostes about the pay deal amounting to a 19 per cent cut for new recruits. On the first day 70 per cent of flights from Heathrow and many from Gatwick were grounded. BA management threats to sue the strikers coincided with a spate of sick notes and more bad publicity; the BMA complaining that BA's policy of demanding that staff obtain a sickness certificate for even one day off was wasting the time of GPs. Catering workers in the TGWU voted 3-1 to reject an offer aimed at making sub-contracting more acceptable. However, the sweeteners had their effect, the ground staff backing away from a strike as shop stewards decided to reopen negotiations. This was small comfort to management because, in general, the paradigmatic change strategy had developed into full-scale confrontation. 'BA is now engaged in the most massive, highly organized and well-funded union-busting operation ever seen in the airline industry,' David Cockcroft, general secretary of the International Transport Federation told members.

It would be impossible to prove. For the necessary paradigmatic or constitutional change, BA management needed a permanent revolution. Yet the lesson of the two summers of strife was that analysis of business strategy cannot be separated from the idea of strategic fit - does the strategy fit into the business environment or terrain facing the company? As chief executive, Bob Ayling wanted sweeping, irreversible change, rather than chipping away at what he perceived as the unions' outdated collective powers and practices. He reckoned that all BA staff should be accountable as individuals shaping the company's competitiveness and profitability as a consensual group of employee-shareholders - marginalizing the unions as, at best, one of many channels of communication.

For the strategy to fit, he needed a crisis; not a crisis in industrial relations as he soon had that. He needed an industrial competitive crisis because 'there is nothing like an external threat to the core of the business to provide the catalyst for fundamental change in management-union relations - a big bang. Ayling's problem was that first, the airline was not facing an acute crisis, so staff did not see why they should make sacrifices. Second, Ayling alienated staff and unions by trying to bring about change with the deadly combination of appalling timing and inflammatory tactics'. (Walters, 1997).

At the time one transport industry consultant commented: 'How could Ayling who aspires to turn BA into the best-managed company in the world have got himself into this fix? He has precipitated a serious conflict at the worst possible time - two months after the election of a Labour government and a Prime Minister who is his personal friend and, just as summer holiday flying approaches its peak. Negotiations should have started last summer, immediately after the pilots' dispute was settled. Besides, some of the problems facing the company, such as losses from bases outside Heathrow and inefficient use of assets - including people and aircraft - have always been there and should have been addressed years ago.' (Walters, 1997).

Incremental Strategic Change at Air France

During the strike of October 1993, ground staff were the most militant group in the stoppage, begun in response to plans to cut bonus pay and terminate 7,000 jobs. They claimed that ground staff were being treated more harshly than cabin crew and pilots. This claim gathered force and opened a fissure in the fragile unity between Air France management and the French government, as air transport minister Bernard Bosson asked the management to begin urgent talks about the allegation. The violent confrontations between strikers attempting to march onto runways and riot police forced the government to pull the strings, destroying any vestige of independence in the nationalized firm's strategy. In essence, the strategic problem at Air France is that privatization is necessary for independence of management action but privatization of a lossmaking airline is not feasible.

In an effort to revitalise its excessively bureaucratic management structure, Christian Blanc divided it into eleven profit centres - from cabin crew to maintenance, each responsible for its own results. At the same time, he appointed Jean-Pierre Courcol, a former publishing director, as managing director of Air Inter. Fearing further rationalization as a result of closer integration with Air France, Air Inter employees were involved in some stoppages. The SNPIT described the appointment as a provocation, accusing Christian Blanc of concentrating power in his own hands.

To progress the integration, he studiously avoided use of the word 'merger' in his six page address to comité d'entreprise representatives in July 1996, speaking rather tortuously of a 'gathering into one company' of Air France and Air France Europe. The original takeover did not look so brilliant as Air France's first operating profit of the 1990s in the year to April 1996 was obliterated by Air Inter's loss over the same period, mainly due to rapid deregulation of the domestic French market as a result of EU competition requirements. Yet there was little alternative to full merger and rationalization. Anticipating this, the union combine of Air France Europe denounced the merger process, demanding negotiations on how to maintain two separate companies, their areas of activity and 11,000 Air France Europe jobs.

Air France senior management had made a desperate effort - with the strategic plan of 1993 (CAP 93) - to prepare the company for the deregulation of the European Union internal market for air transport in

April 1997. However, this had been abandoned and replaced by incremental change - the only strategy that would fit with the considerable constraints of effective trade union opposition. Hence the official beginning of deregulated open skies in the EU whereby any airline could offer flights between any two EU airports, opening up the French domestic market, was accompanied by strikes of Air France Europe employees. First the pilots began a series of strikes and their action was followed by ground staff.

For Blanc, although he stated that the global airline industry was undergoing revolutionary change, there was no possibility of an espoused strategy of paradigmatic strategic change. That was one strategic choice - to turn Air France into a low-cost airline. Here he did try to conjure up a strategic threat because that choice would mean cutting cots by 30-40 per cent by buying or leasing low-cost aircraft through rudimentary reservation and distribution systems, low pay for employees and withdrawal from many of the activities of a traditional airline. 'Why is that impossible for a traditional company like ours ? For a simple reason. The social cost of such an adjustment would be insupportable.' (Milner, 1996). So, in contrast to Bob Ayling of BA, the espoused strategy tended to accept the legitimacy of responsible trade unionism, although Blanc did lecture the comité d'entreprise that the full merger would remove the crippling uncertainty brought on by vetoing powers of Air France Europe's labour unions and guarantee that Air France as a whole would be turned round by the spring of 1997. To do so, he would have to cut costs at Air France Europe where pilots were reportedly the highest paid in Europe with salaries about 15 per cent above those of Air France pilots. Under a full merger, the salaries would be equalized.

In June 1998, Air France pilots again took strike action against management plans to trim the annual cost of their pay by FFr500 million. They claimed to have had real salary cuts of 30 per cent over the previous 15 years and resented being asked for further concessions when the company was returning to profitability. With the Football World Cup being held in France, the SNPL felt strong enough to mount a 'strategic' strike. Union leaders representing other grades of employee did not support the strike but threatened that any more concessions to the pilots would invite comparability as there were already wild cat actions by ground staff.

Mindful of a repetition of the compromises of 1993 and 1995, the Jospin government decided to back the hard line of the management. At first it looked as though there was going to be appeasement in view of the threat of transport chaos during the World Cup. However, trade unionism also depends on feelings of equity and the conviction grew among other Air France employees that the SNPL had dangerously overplayed its apparently strong hand. They began to accuse the pilots of blackmail and of threatening the livelihoods of other employees. Four smaller unions representing pilots broke ranks and offered a compromise agreement. Moreover, the brinkmanship had the paradoxical effect that, as the strikes had already happened, little more damage could be done to the reputation of Air France - or the commercial image of France. In fact, some credibility would probably be restored by taking a tougher line. This tough line was vindicated when the pilots ended the strike by accepting terms no better - and possibly less favourable - than those that they had rejected a week earlier, involving shares for a pay freeze.

Constitutional Change and Industrial Relations Strategy

So what can be said about industrial relations strategy at BA and Air France? Constitutional or paradigmatic strategic change was attempted at BA and appeared to fit with the global strategy. However, decision-making failed to properly take account of 'the organizational aspects of the decision process, including the very important challenges to management's right to a unilateral role. (Chandler:258). There were three fundamental challenges to the union presence: a compression of pay and benefits differentials for pilots; a opening up of the pay gap between present cabin staff and new recruits that threatened future earnings, and, the contracting out of some ground staff tasks. Although the challenge to contracting out melted away, the union had been able to gain concessions for the ground staff affected. In the end, management had to collectively bargain and reach settlements, the very facets of human resource management that the purported strategy had sought to avoid. At a stormy AGM just after the cabin crew strike, 'BA's board was harangued over its new corporate style' (Pain, 1997) and investing institutions grew anxious about the confrontational approach. It was necessary to trim back strategy to a more incremental human resource management.

Air France senior management had long since abandoned the revolutionary, paradigmatic change that had been attempted with CAP 93. Paradoxically, however, their more incremental approach, involving collective bargaining separately with Air France Europe staff, encouraged the pilots union to bite off more than it could chew, implying coercion rather than the resistance of traditional union ideology and thereby losing the support of other employees. The management tried to avoid direct talk of merger. In fact the full merger was enough to provide the unitary message that was all that was required to bring a settlement when the pilots union overplayed its hand.

Values and ideology have been important in these defeats for organized labour. Under the influence of a recrudescence of neoclassical economic doctrine, unions and procedures have been character assassinated as obstrusive rigidities. Actually, procedures for handling redundancy in particular have been far from rigid. Strategic management, entrusted with rescuing airlines and rationalizing to cut costs, has caricatured older industrial relations procedures as bureaucratic. It has to be said that actions, such as that of the French pilots' union help sustain this image. To pursue efficiency, strategic management has decreed that there has to be flexibility and, ostensibly, decentralisation. In fact, there has been more use of centralised personnel groups, often now called human resource management, in a changing workplace. Superficially, human resource management has been mocked as industrial relations without unions. Less facetiously, human resource management has been constructed as a kind of field officer class of strategic management, responsible for chivvying line management to raise productivity. In another way of looking at this, Kochan and Capelli (1984) expected that the 'distinction between labour relations, human resource management and operating management will become increasingly blurred as firms attempt simultaneously to control production costs, increase employee communications and involvement, maintain stable union-management relations where unions exist and avoid new opportunities for union organizing.'

The form that this has taken has often been decentralisation, though the actual result is often centralisation. At Air France, centralizing moves were cloaked in rhetoric of decentralization. Hence the proposed full merger with Air France Europe clearly drew attention to the gap between decentralizing rhetoric and the reality of further rationalization. In industrial relations generally, decentralization has been palpable in pay determination, with moves to individualized, performance-related pay and real pay cuts. However, its main manifestation has been through outsourcing and sub-contracting. In the very high pay-off strategies, sub-contracting is envisaged as releasing carriers to focus on core competencies – transporting passengers. For really high value-added, this may be distilled to a focus on business class passengers. 'The third phase of post-privatization development will see BA increasingly turned into a business-class airline flying point-to-point passengers.' (Harrison, 1999). Sub-contracting is seen here as an external form of devolution of administration, avoiding the costs and burdens of managing a complex internal labour market – and potentially avoiding the concessions required when managers are obliged to recognize and bargain in good faith with unions. Nevertheless, there are limits to functional flexibility for the 50 per cent of airline employees who work as flight attendants, cabin crew and engineers, owing to international regulations, crewing requirements for particular aircraft and, to some extent, work practices. Managements may want to operate as 'virtual airlines' – as businesses with few elements of organization. However, as pointed out by Chandler in her book *Management Rights and Union Interests*, this is very much a constitutional issue and one which can shatter the psychological contract with possibly damaging consequences. Is it the fact that 'in the end, wholly dependent on good employee morale, management, in any circumstances, are largely constrained in their actions'? (Warhurst, 1996:274).

Since much of the change process has actually been towards more centralized control (with budgetary controls laid down by head office), the task for human resource management has been to reconcile tough action by senior management to cut jobs with the need for motivation to increase productivity and maintain quality of service, even as numbers employed fall. Just as industrial relations procedures until the last quarter of the century were transparent and rather mechanistic, so human resource management tends to be opaque and in fact to operate as a smokescreen. Real pay and conditions for many categories of airline personnel have deteriorated. Among flight attendants in particular, now and in the conceivable future, it would be hard to find one to describe the job as either glamorous in the old sense or as well-paid with reasonable conditions as it was in the recent past.

It could not be argued that the constitutional change in industrial relations extends to the elimination of industrial conflict, as some human resource management theorists have suggested. Recession and global excess capacity with resultant job cuts have put employees in a weak position to resist deteriorating terms and conditions, including sub-contracting. This is not to say, however, that these constitutional changes are considered acceptable by employees or their organisations who are very much on the receiving end of human resource management 'improvements'. Once the importance of strategy is accepted, there is a danger that those who oppose any strategy, good or bad, can be scapegoated for an enterprise's problems.

The 'Virtual Strike' Held at Meridiana Airline

Unions are increasingly aware of this and of the need to avoid being seen as obstuctionist and anti-consumer. In a peculiar example in July 1999, during negotiations over the collective agreement at Meridiana, Italy's largest private airline operating domestic and European routes and employing some 1,500 workers. Pilots belonging to two national occupational unions for pilots, proposed that a half-day strike already called fro 27 July should be transformed into a 'virtual strike'. They proposed this form of industrial action in a letter sent to the chair of the authority for the enforcement of the law on strikes in essential public services and to the Italian Minister of Transport. The letter referred explicitly to Italy's 1998 *Pact on concertation policies and on new rules in industrial relations* for the transport industry. The Pact, among other things, envisages forms of collective action that 'although onerous for the enterprises and for the workers who take part in the protest, do not affect provision of the service and do not penalize users'.

The Minister was positive about the proposal and, following his mediation, Meridiana accepted the pilots' proposal and undertook to donate the receipts from flights occurring during the hours of the 'virtual strike' to humanitarian organizations. The parties also agreed to comply with an arbitration award to be issued by the Minister that would define the amount to be paid by the company. The strike was then joined by cabin crew belonging to CGIL who preferred to call this kind of alternative action 'solidaristic', in order to apply pressure for renewal of the company agreement covering flight attendants which was being negotiated at the same time as the pilots' deal. As a result, there was no disruption of Meridiana's flights, passengers being notified by cabin crew that their flights would not be affected because the strike was being carried out 'virtually', although those taking part wore a white bow on their sleeves to display their participation.

Although in principle one may share the Transport Minister's positive reception for the virtual strike, in practice there are significant problems. Firstly, how is worker participation – and hence deduction and donation of wages – to be verified? There is the risk of free-riding. There is already fragmented union representation in airlines and further fragmentation might be encouraged. From the company's point of view, a virtual strike may be more costly than a conventional strike. The Meridiana pilots' original demand – considered unacceptable by the company – was for 100 per cent of all receipts to be donated to humanitarian organizations. Possibly company costs should be calculated on the basis of profits but if so, what should be done in the case of public service enterprises that operate at a loss ? (Pedersini,1999).

Espoused strategies of globalization, such as that of BA, may be constrained by the bilateral character of air services agreements between national governments, except in single market trading areas such as the European Union. Even then, national governments have been able to negotiate safeguards and some protection for their flag carriers, though in 1998 state support for Air France was deemed over the agreed limit by the European Court. Nevertheless, the fundamental issue is that airline companies are faced by global markets for nearly all grades of labour. National-level industrial relations institutions are otiose and national governments have tended to undermine them, directly or by benign neglect.

Consequently, rather than considering recent industrial relations country-by-country, the crucial nature of this chapter for the entire book is dramatised by its expansion into part III of four parts. The remainder of this part will discuss the constitutional changes in industrial relations by reference to four of the main occupational categories among employees - maintenance engineers, pilots and flight attendants, and, ground staff. In the first three categories, the idea of the craft and occupational professionalism have been under attack as airline managements have aimed to cut pay costs and raise productivity by emphasising flexibility and dissolving collective bargaining by organized labour, as was suggested by the general secretary of the International Transport Federation during the BA cabin crew dispute in 1997. (Milne, 1997).

Maintenance and Engineering Workers

In many industries, maintenance and repair is an obvious area where numerical flexibility can be introduced by means of sub-contracting. As the ILO report (1990) put it, 'extensive computerization and greater reliance on electronics in aircraft components and in testing and maintenance equipment have paralleled the changes in aircraft technology. Information on the operation and health of all aircraft systems during flight and on any malfunctions is stored on a floppy disk. The disk is available to engineers on the ground who quickly identify any problem. In addition, 'integrated digital testing equipment enables a single person to test entire systems in a matter of minutes. Most parts and components are no longer repaired by the airline but are sent to the manufacturer for that purpose'. (ILO,1990:28).

However, it has already been pointed out that there are obvious hostages to fortune in contracting out maintenance in that it may not pay to rely on maintenance facilities that are in the hands of competitors. Even if they are not in the hands of close competitors, an airline may find that its maintenance schedules are not being met because of the contractor's troubled industrial relations, as was the case when the Team subsidiary of Aer Lingus was shackled by go-slow and working to rule in opposition to planned job cuts.

Aircraft maintenance workers figured in the fictional airline "Blue Star" in the film *Wall Street* which dramatised the asset stripping and rationalisation of the actual industry. In the USA, airline bargaining has only rarely if, ever, approached the archetypal pre-constitutional industrial relations change position of national bargaining. Rather, collective bargaining by airlines tended to be relatively uncoordinated. There were some elements of a constitutional national centralised bargaining framework. In 1936, the airline industry was placed by Congress under the Railway Labour Act - a law designed specifically to cover railroad labour relations. The law established the National Mediation Board that was responsible for attempting to bring about settlement of any dispute that threatened to interrupt interstate commerce and in a sense predetermined the type of bargaining units that would develop.

Nevertheless, despite some pressures towards multi-carrier collective bargaining, co-ordinated bargaining was always spasmodic. The experiments with multi-carrier bargaining indicated the long-standing interest of airline managements in arriving at some cohesive system whereby settlements would depend not so much on the expediency of competitive gain or of keeping the business operating as an well thought-out and practical long term objectives. In 1958, however, the industry experienced a series of strikes and labour emergencies that tended to highlight the unequal strength enjoyed by the unions and the highly divisive forces pressuring management.

Deregulation in the 1970s switched interest away from co-ordinated bargaining. Even the slight pattern and centralizing factors of national mediation were dropped by President Bush in 1989. Ignoring advice from the National Mediation Board, the Bush administration, through its tough Transportation Secretary, Samuel Skinner, refused to declare an a emergency that would have postponed the strike at Eastern Airlines for 60 days, arguing that there was no guarantee that the 17 month dispute would be resolved after the 'cooling-off period'. Bush became the first President to reject a Mediation board recommendation to intervene in a labour dispute. Frank Lorenzo had taken over Eastern Airlines through his holding company, Texas Air Corporation. Having previously forced his flagship carrier, Continental Airlines, into bankruptcy to defeat the unions, he had attacked the 8,500 strong International Association of Machinists, the last remaining group of workers resisting pay cuts and flexibility. Lorenzo's antipathy to unions is illustrated by the following remarks made in a rare interview in the respected monthly magazine, 'Airline Business':

'The unions went to everybody who flew Eastern and said that Eastern was unsafe. They have scared all the high yield traffic away from Eastern. They have created a loss environment at Eastern. We sell assets and they scream some more and call us asset strippers because we have to sell assets to finance the losses'.

The strike of 8,500 maintenance workers was supported by a majority of Eastern's 3,500 pilots and 5,900 flight attendants. Eastern executives were forced to admit that they had underestimated the strength of support of the pilots for the engineers and maintenance workers' union.

In a contrasting presidential policy, Clinton persuaded American Airlines to accept binding arbitration of its dispute with flight attendants in 1993. In another more peacefully, though tortuously, negotiated episode of the employee buy-out of United Airlines, the engineering union was the most recusant. The initiative came from the unions and marked a profound change in management - labour relations which had been strained since 1991. In the final agreement, UAL's employees exchanged pay cuts and work rule concessions for a majority stake in the carrier. The deal was temporarily stalled when the engineering union objected to the concessions that its members would have to make and demanded that management and non-contract employees make bigger concessions.

Flight Attendants

Flight attendants would not be in a very strong bargaining position anyway, irrespective of the over-capacity and intensified competition among airline companies. They and their unions have to decide whether to cooperate with management and how far to accept changes in terms of employment. Numerical flexibility means that they will have to deal with the increasing numbers of temporary staff who may or may not readily join or be willingly accepted by unions. At any event, the representative status of unions has been reduced and many of the industrial disputes involving flight attendants have reflected this. They tend to form rather erratic work groups, to use the ancient terminology of Sayles (1958), in that they may take industrial action from time to time to protect their interests but it is transient and not concerted enough; the advent of the two-tier pay structure has exacerbated this tendency.

As elsewhere, it seems, some managers may talk about human resource management performance appraisal and total quality management but, for those at the receiving end, the injection of market-based merit pay to demean experience is resented. A flight attendant with United Airlines said that what women in the industry were seeing was an attempt by the companies to say 'we have yet thousands of 20-year olds who could do the job' and that is a real attack on the self-esteem of the worker. (Mackie, 1987).

In all this, the idea that flight attendants are crucial when things go wrong in an aircraft has suffered. When flight attendants work longer hours, have short turn-round periods and see their training programme cut, as well as being locked in combat with their employers, they do not even try to pretend that safety aspects are the major part of their job. It is now impossible to describe the flight attendant's job as glamorous in any sense or as well paid with reasonable conditions. In recent years, low pay and lengthened hours - with a guerrilla war to retain what has not so far been lost - provide a better description.

There has been resistance by unions to the flexibility plans of management as during the 1997 BA strike. The TGWU continued to resist contracting cut and the transfer of work to subsidiaries offering worse pay and conditions but it has been in too weak a bargaining position to do very much. The strike was weakened by inter-union rivalry between the TGWU and Cabin Crew '89, a breakaway for long-haul staff recognized in that year by BA. In March 1999, the sectionalism worsened when members of Cabin Crew '89 voted overwhelmingly to merge with the AEEU, an arch-rival of the TGWU. The TGWU leadership, already vexed with the AEEU for gaining recognition at BA's cut-price airline, Go, reacted angrily. Bill Morris, TGWU general secretary, said that Cabin Crew '89 was a breakaway union and therefore the AEEU, as a TUC affiliate, should not be allowed to merge with it.

Perhaps the most surprising opposition to management cost-cutting came from the 17 day strike of Cathay Pacific flight attendants in 1993. Cathay, controlled by the Swire Pacific Group whose management was dominated by British and Australian expatriates, often accused of a patronising attitude towards their mainly Asian staff, was certainly not expecting a strike. The strike was sparked by plans for cost cutting measures. Specifically, although the union had made significant concessions, its leaders refused to end the strike when Cathay management said that strike activists would be disciplined. As one of the world's three most profitable airlines, they believed that there was no necessity for Cathay to take such a tough line. Later, Rod Eddington, the Cathay managing director, proposed an audit of external and internal communications, a response typical of the unitary perspective on employee relations: 'A particular management challenge is how to communicate with an absent workforce, with so many of them away (from Hong Kong) at any one time. We have a new member of the management specifically to communicate with the cabin crew community - sod's law applies, he was arriving just as the strike began'. (Westlake, 1993). However, many of the airline's employees complained that much more needed to be done: 'If they put in someone whom the crews can trust, the relationship will improve in time', said one, 'but the management has to bend over backwards to show they are sincere and now that they have lost all their trust and respect, it's not going to be easy'. (Westlake, 1993).

The costs of the strike to Cathay were substantial. The airline admitted to losing up to $2 million a day during the first 10 days of the strike, well timed to coincide with a holiday period. Based on its results for the first half of 1992, Cathay could have reckoned on daily profits of about U.S. $1 million from normal operations. The public relations and marketing damage of pictures of large numbers of young women chanting slogans outside the airline's offices was also significant. In the event, profits plunged almost fifty per cent for the first half of 1993.

The strike reflected one of the universals in the changing constitution of employee relations in the industry - the attack on professionalism and staff status which has become an empty phrase. The Flight Attendants' Union instruction to its members to strike was not directly about money. Having complained in November 1992 that the airline was understaffed - with the result that flight attendants sometimes had to 'workdown' by doing more menial tasks in order to cover for junior staff - the union instructed members on 7 December to refuse future requests to work below their rank. Three cabin attendants who followed this instruction were subsequently suspended on 12 December and sacked 2 days later, whereupon the union pressed for reinstatement and called the strike. In the circumstances, one suggestion to avoid future conflict - more deregulation - seemed singularly inappropriate since it would intensify competition and cause further pressure on pay and conditions of service (Westlake, 1993). In the event, there were some job cuts and allegations of victimization.

Pilots

Of all the categories of airline employed, pilots have traditionally held the greatest claim to professional status. Until the deflationary and deregulated era of the last quarter century they have also generally been in a strong position to enforce it by virtue of their relative scarcity. The necessarily prolonged and stringent training required ensured such scarcity until deregulation and intensified competition and the excess airline capacity induced by recession altered the balance of supply and demand. In addition, it is now technologically possible to fly and navigate aircraft without humans at the controls, though acceptance of this by passengers is another matter.

In his then definitive work on airline management, W.S. Barry noted in 1965 that 'to emphasise the need to maintain strict standards, pilots sometimes refer to their job as a profession. They may hope to acquire some of the traditional status of the law, church and medicine. But it is as well to remember that these three occupations are called professions because those who practice them make a public avowal of faith in certain principles. The lawyer's belief in the rule of law, the doctor's belief in the sanctity of human life and the church's belief in God are uncompromising to a degree that a pilot could not maintain in, say, promoting safety. Pilots should not be encouraged to take a 'holier-than-business' attitude to their daily work. It is safer for pilots to regard their job as a craft that is exercised for profit but which demands exceptional skills in pursuit of the perfection aimed at by good crafts workers.' (Barry, 1965:152). As professional status among pilots has been devalued by the injection of business management techniques and market relations, this precept can be seen to have been well-founded. However, nor have the three learned professions escaped disturbance of their autonomy by the rigours of the market.

Pilots are faced by employers who have a global labour market from which to draw their recruitment. Although globalization strategies have so far been hampered by the essentially national and bilateral regulatory governing structure of air transport, nonetheless there are inchoate moves towards 'open skies' in the Luxembourg agreement by the governments of the European Union, by the US Transportation Department in negotiation with other national governments, and, by the partial formation of megacarriers. Such companies might find it advantageous to play off one set of flight crews against another, particularly where their operations straddle national boundaries. The easier it becomes to transfer flight crews between the countries of the European Union or to import them from non-member countries, the stronger becomes the employers' bargaining power.

In response to this industrial challenge, 20,000 pilots in the 12 European Union countries, were brought together in the European Cockpit Association, the result of a joint initiative by the British and German pilots' unions in 1990 (Harper, 1990). Unlike other international trade union associations, the intention was to make this one into a genuine negotiating body. Despite this there has been little evidence of international solidarity among pilots even in Europe.

Training requirements for pilots are onerous, particularly in the UK, thereby restricting supply somewhat. The minimum requirement for a commercial pilot's licence is 700 flying hours plus the Air Law examination and an Instrument Rating Flight Test. Nevertheless, the drop in demand relative to supply in the early 1990s could be illustrated by reference to the fact that BA had 280 fully qualified cadet pilots who had graduated from Oxford Air Training school or from Prestwick but who could not be given a job in 1992. Since qualifying as commercial pilots, some cadets had taken jobs outside the industry or were employed as stewards at a basic salary of £7,800 compared to £25,000 that they would have earned as co-pilots. Some were then being recruited by Cathay Pacific to fly jumbo jets. They would not be allowed to handle the aircraft below 10,000 feet and so should not be at the controls at take off or landing. Nevertheless, they were needed to monitor the instruments of long-haul Boeing 747s while the main crew rested during non-stop flights between Hong Kong and Europe.

In the USA in 1999, a senior pilot at American Airlines could expect to work about 14 days a month and could earn more than $200,000 a year. Forced by federal law to retire at 60, that pilot receives a lifelong pension and a lump-sum payment that can reach $3 million. Although among the best-paid, they are among the most militant in pay bargaining. Members of a skilled elite, pilots exhibit a strong self-confidence and can be likened to strategic work groups. "They really think that they are at the centre of the universe," said an executive at a major US airline who regularly negotiates with the pilots and therefore insisted on anonymity. "They are people who are trained to think in terms of right and wrong. They are not trained to tolerate ambiguity." (Zuckerman,1999).

American Airlines pilots were due to go on strike in March 1997 until President Clinton used his emergency powers to order them back to work for a 60 day 'cooling-off' period. The dispute was not so much about more money as about the threat to established pay and conditions by dilution as a result of transferring pilots from other airlines. Bob Crandall, then the American Chief Executive, had ordered that the airline's new regional jets could be flown only by lower-paid pilots from another union. Naturally, the regular pilots did not want to be told which planes they could or could not fly –as this would seem to impugn their professional status. Not only that but they were concerned lest the newer pilots took their jobs.

The dispute had the rest of the industry loooking on nervously. Regional jets (RJs) are the biggest innovation to affect air travel since the super wide-body was introduced in the early 1980s. Since deregulation of the industry, the big companies have been investing in feeder services to compete with upstart airlines such as Southwest. With 50-70 seat RJs, the market is transformed but to keep their costs and pay off the investment, some of the larger carriers told their pilots to expect pay cuts if they want to fly RJs. For example, to avoid the union contract assuring pilots of flying any plane with 60 seats or more, Northwest ordered twelve 59-seat RJs.

Among the aggravating factors in the American Airlines dispute was the lack of trust in Robert Crandall. Pilots did not trust him because of continuous attempts at dilution of their pay and conditions. They expected him to violate the spirit of any agreement. However, by 1999 Crandall had retired, yet the pilots were in dispute once again. This time the ostensible issue was how the company was going to integrate the pay and conditions of staff at Reno Air, bought in December 1998. The pilots suspected that this was the latest in the series of tactical moves designed to squeeze more work out of them and erode their job security. They accused American of violating the clause in their contract that guaranteed that all flying at American would be done by members of their union, the Allied Pilots Association. The 300 pilots at Reno Air were represented by the rival Air Line Pilots Association and their pay was considerably lower.

Wary of the 'cooling off' period imposed during the 1997 dispute, the union held back but hundreds of American pilots stayed off work, calling in as sick. Under US labour law, the union could not avoid being deemed responsible. The pilots returned to work after a federal judge cited the union for contempt and for disobeying his order to end the 'sick-out'. He chided the pilots for the trivial cause of the dispute, calling their sick-out a shakedown worthy of organized crime, and ordered the union to set aside $10 million for damages.

'Pilots have never been an easy group for airline executives to deal with. To a large degree, their exalted status is reinforced by the travelling public. One major airline recently surveyed public attitudes towards pilots' pay and found that most people were not offended that pilots were making $200,000 a yeaar. Those surveyed felt that pilots, like heart surgeons, should be well compensated because they wanted to see those professions attract the most competent people. Yet, at the same time, the job itself has become more mundane. Commercial jets have become more automated, requiring less actual flying skill.' (Zuckerman, 1999).

The decline in the professional status of pilots has not been replicated everywhere. It has been reported that the pilots' union in Russia has sought to consolidate the position of its members as a labour aristocracy, collaborating closely with management to secure its privileged position. (Borisov, 1994). There the success of the pilots was contrasted with the heavy defeat suffered by the air traffic controllers following their strikes in August and December 1992. In general, however, pilots' unions have been unable to resist the constitutional change in airline industrial relations. We may therefore agree with Capelli (1985) that numerous factors affect a craft's ability to resist deregulatory competitive pressures and that deregulatory effects on pilots may not be as pervasive as commonly believed, though it is harder to accept that there is 'not much evidence' that crafts previously captured regulatory rents.

Ground Staff

The category of airline employees least likely to be perceived as skilled and whose supply is virtually limitless is ground staff. Specifically, we mean aircraft cleaning staff and baggage handling staff. To some extent, the latter may be employed by the airport authority or company. However, there must always be a residual who are employed by or contracted by the airline company, though historically baggage handling and aircraft maintenance have been contracted out by all but the largest airlines. A certain airline once had all its apron services at its main base carried out by the airport authority. The airline then took all the staff employed on this work into its own organisation. Management reckoned that this would save money because the same volume of business was now being done by a larger organisation. But capacity tonne-miles per employee, an important measure of productivity, dropped. In the recessionary era of the 1980s and 1990s, companies tend to want to increase contracting and concentrate on core activities with the same amount of work being done.

However, loading and unloading passengers' baggage requires care and control. It is an area for Total Quality Management because errors that, on the face of it, may seem trivial to an airline employee may be perceived as much more serious by the person whose comfort and convenience may be seriously disturbed for days. This was an important factor in the demise of People Express, after brief success as a low cost, no frills airline.

This threat - amidst what is for many customers a stressful type of travel anyway - does indirectly give ground staff some kind of bargaining power. It is the brute force from ability to disrupt the smooth arrival of passengers and their belongings or the threat to do so. BA broke a strike of ground staff in the early 1980s, effectively atrophying their industrial muscle and they were quiescent during the 1997 disputes. The most notable dispute involving ground staff in recent years was that at Ryanair in March 1998. Fewer than 40 members of the SIPTU (Services, Industrial, Professional and Technical Union) employed as ground-handling agents, i.e. baggage handlers, pressed for recognition of their union by Ryanair. Management refused point blank to countenance recognition, the union reacting by enagaging in industrial action involving the relatively small number of employees. The dispute escalated, leading to the closedown of Dublin airport. A special two-member inquiry appointed by the Irish government, found that primary responsibility rested with both the SIPTU and the management of the Ryanair airline. The report of an enquiry by the government into the general issue of trade union recognition, having advocated continuation of Ireland's voluntarist tradition, was rather knocked back by the ferocity of the Ryan dispute.

Summing up on Union Activity

The airline industry's volatility results in many revealing episodes of conflict between management and unions. In spite of considerable union penetration and extensive membership, the fragmented structure of the industry due to deregulation makes solidarity vital. Unfortunately, from the union viewpoint, solidarity is hardly characteristic of inter-union relationships in the industry. Rather, inter-union rivalry and poaching of members have been commonplace. In certification contests in the USA much effort is expended for a limited return (Walsh, 1994) and union ties in the industry are hardly characterized by solidarity as union rivalries and raiding have been pervasive. In the UK, the establishment of cut-price, no frills airlines has led to 'beauty contests' where unions display their willingness to make concessionary agreements. (Clements, 1998).

The Importance of Industrial Relations for Human Resource Management

The importance of industrial relations for human resource management was underlined during the summer of 1999 by the appointment of Speedwing, the consulting arm of BA, to manage Olympic Airways. The Greek government appointed Speedwing following the collapse of restructuring and rationalization attempts in the previous four years. Olympic's 18 unions, notably militant pilots and cabin crews, undermined cost-cutting efforts and forced the resignation of three chief executives. Consequently, a senior Olympic executive admitted that 'labour relations have to be top of the agenda. For years the unions have been more powerful than the managers. They are becoming less militant but there is still opposition to overcome from flight engineers and technical maintenance staff.' (Hope, 1999). In fact, OSPA, the union federation, had immediately declared its opposition to the appointment of a foreign manager. However, its threat to stage strikes throughout the tourist season only served to further improve bookings with Olympic's local competitors. For BA, the contract was a curious one to take on – they defeated competition from American, United and Lufthansa – given the wounds inflicted on them in recent strikes by their own employees. Perhaps the Greek government believed that they were battle-hardened and ready for the 30 month contract of £7 million with the further incentive of a stake of up to 20 per cent if Olympic could be returned to profitability and privatized. In August 2000, the finance ministry, Olympic's only shareholder, ended the contract after BA declined its option to buy 20 per cent of Olympic.

PART IV
HUMAN RESOURCE
MANAGEMENT AND OTHER
MANAGEMENT FUNCTIONS

Introduction to Chapters 8, 9 and 10

A key aspiration of human resource management is to be strategic. This is a matter of some difficulty when 'strategy' is so hard to define or when it means more or less what Quality Assurance consultants say it means. However, in relation to management, it appears to entail being able to anticipate developments, rather than merely reacting to them. It is part of scenario-building (Piganiol, 1989). It is also means that, rather than being a separate specialist administrative function, human resource management is intended to be integrated throughout management in general. There is a great danger of the ostensible tenet of human resource management that 'people are central to the business' becoming a shibboleth.

On the evidence of business strategies used by managements of nearly all commercial airlines in recent years, it is realistic rather than cynical to say that integrating human resource management into general management means making the human resources fit in with priority decisions, primarily marketing decisions. The industry has suffered from considerable over-capacity and market-led decisions have often been alongside rationalization and job cuts. It would be a mission impossible to find a large airline company that had not cut jobs in the 1990s.

The upshot of the integration of human resource management into general management at one time seemed likely to lead to a diminution of the power and influence of the specialist professional personnel manager. It is true, as can be deduced from the previous section on industrial relations, that the functional need for such professionals to interpret the rules of collective bargaining and industrial conflict and to 'hold the ring' between employer and trade union has been much reduced. Nevertheless, the injection of the market deeper into the airline organisation calls for some erstwhile personnel management functions to be actually enhanced in importance. In particular, great attention to customer care and Total Quality Management logically entail more rigorous and systematic recruitment and training policies.

The assimilation of production management by market relations under the banner of human resource management is discussed in this section's opening chapter (8). There follows a discussion of the all-important financial capital base and its influence on human resource management in chapter 9. Finally the continuing procedural and ever-present employee welfare concerns of personnel management are addressed in chapter 10 which also attempts to summarise the issues covered in this book. It also shows the limitations to the integration of human resource management in a strategic sense. Finance, marketing and, to a lesser extent, production have primary – with human resource management appearing and evanescing as mainly tactical. The variability of training policies, inconsistent attitudes to participation and opportunist pay settlements, such as at Ryanair, strongly indicate the one-sidedness of any strategic human resource management.

8 Airline Production Management and Human Resource Management

Production is about adding value with a view to realising that gain when the product is marketed and purchased by customers. The product of air transport is, more than anything, the arrival of passengers or freight. Airlines are producing arrivals of passengers, freight and mail. According to the ILO Report of 1990 on structural change in aviation, 'the most important development in this area has been the growth of computerized reservation systems (CRS) as comprehensive marketing tools.' (ILO:29).

Most airlines do indeed associate reservations systems with the marketing function. If the product is 'arrivals', however, the seats and freight space flown through the air can be regarded as equipment in use. 'Whether the equipment is productive or not depends on whether it is used on raw materials, i.e. passengers or freight. Reservations, therefore, are of equipment and not of stock. The word reservation conveys the idea of keeping something for a certain purpose. This, however, is much too passive a notion of what really happens in making airline reservations. Here it is a matter of allocating a passenger to a certain flight (after seeing that there is room for her) and then guiding her by various means to that flight. In the circumstances, 'passenger-allocations' would be a more meaningful term than reservations. Seen in this light, the task of reservations properly belongs to the functions of passenger and freight control' (Barry: 248) and therefore is part of the process of production. Computerized reservation systems play an important role in what airline owners call 'inventory control' or maximising revenues from each seat. In conditions of over-capacity airlines have struggled to cut prices sufficiently to sell seats on competitive routes while keeping them high enough to make a profit.

A crucial effect of information technology in such uses as CRS is in reducing the disequilibrium between market demand and production and therefore between marketing and production management.

'Of similar importance in the competitive environment has been the development of yield-management systems whose function is to gather and analyse data on passenger demand for each flight and extrapolate optimal fares, in other words, those yielding the highest revenues for each flight. In addition to giving airlines that use these techniques a competitive edge over their rivals, the decisive advantage of these systems lies in providing airline management with real-time data on changing market trends and enabling it immediately to adapt capacity, schedules and prices in response to such trends. For example, these systems have been the determining tool in enabling airlines to better competitors' discounts by using marginal costing techniques.' (ILO:29).

Costs

Although CRS and yield management systems are really technology and techniques that are logically under the remit of production management in airlines, there seems little point in trying to turnback the tide that has expanded the marketing function to encompass and colonize such tools. Even Air France, at one time a notably production-oriented organization, has shifted to widening its marketing/commercial function. What really alarmed Bernard Attali, company president until his resignation in protest against government appeasement of the unions during the strike of 1993, about competing mega-carriers, such as American and United, was their control over CRUs. It was no accident that the first strategic plan was called CAP 93 because this reflected the acronym for computer-aided production.

In many ways this development is unfortunate for the old-style production function. Previously principally about sequencing, it is now reduced to concern about costs. Any strategic possibilities for production management seem destined for the management of change that has been colonized by human resource management. This is not to say that operating costs are not important in airlines. However, as the economist Doganis has very well elucidated, management control over costs in airlines is often constrained. Obviously there is total control over marketing, product planning and financial policy. This goes without saying as these result from overall strategic decisions, such as about whether to expand and diversify or contract to a market niche. Sir Michael Bishop of British Midland avoided taking on giant operators on their long haul routes and kept out of the package holiday business. He also astutely bought up slots at Heathrow when they became available. Air France and BA took the decision to expand, initially by takeover. Such decisions affect future strategy, so although under complete control in principle, set a framework that then dictates what can be controlled and what cannot.

The type of aircraft and the pattern of operations where the aircraft are used are determinants of costs where management has somewhat less control. Discretion may be limited by previous decisions. Examples are bilateral air services agreements negotiated by the government. BA's business strategy was dented by the authorities' decision to increase competition into Heathrow and by lapses in the Air Services Agreement with the USA that permitted a continued high level of protection of the US internal market.

The geographical location of an airline's home base is a factor that can dictate costs. Sometimes this element is not as fixed as it seems and a drastic upheaval can symbolize and precipitate necessary organizational change, as in the Air France migration from central Paris to Charles de Gaulle airport.

An apparent area for manoeuvre on production costs is revealed by the rise in aircraft leasing, whereby, instead of buying aircraft outright, airlines lease them from a third party. An issue of finance, rather than production management, aircraft leasing is discussed in chapter 9. Apart from its applications for yield management, the internet has brought possible economies in purchasing. BA combined with five other airlines to start an internet marketplace to handle around $32bn in annual purchasing. The network will cover the procurement of key products, such as fuel, engines and maintenance services. (Cope, 2000).

A third area where airlines have limited control over costs includes elements such as prevailing pay levels, fuel prices and airport charges. For an airline business, these are more or less given. 'Wage costs are 25-35 per cent of total operating costs for most airlines, though the figure is lower for many Third World airlines. The Asian carriers, except JAL, pay very low wages for all categories of staff when compared with most international competitors. To ensure their future profitability, international airlines must first of all significantly reduce their labour costs to levels that are comparable to those of the newer Asian carriers. This means by increases in labour productivity.' (Doganis, 1991:345). Airlines, such as Singapore Airlines, that have both relatively low wage levels and high productivity are in a very strong competitive position.

According to Jean-Louis Morisot, regional transportation analyst for Goldman Sachs in Singapore, 'the focus on internals is necessary because the immense pressure on yields is not going to go away. The only way to grow earnings is through cost-cutting and with labour costs, they have only just scratched the surface'. (Chow, 1997). Seristo (1996) agreed with this view in his analysis of survey a of European airline managers to ascertain how they perceive the cost problem. He reported that all managers expected cost pressures to continue and that drastic changes are required. Declining yields were perceived as the biggest problem area. High salaries and benefits, inflexible work rules and the inflexible attitude of trade unions were seen as major contributors to cost problems. This bleak outlook was broadly endorsed by Robert Ayling in his first major speech since being ousted as chief executive of BA: 'If we don't get a new round of productivity jumps, there are going to be some major catastrophes in the airline world.' (Harrison, 2000).

Together with Vepsalainen, Seristo (1997) extended his work to analyse factors driving airline costs, in particular the implications for fleet, routes and personnel policies. Their analysis discovered that the utilization rates of flight personnel do differ quite significantly from one airline to another. As personnel costs in total typically represent 25-35 per cent of an airline's total operating costs – the flying personnel being particularly expensive – the authors considered that it is important for an airline to obtain as much work input from the personnel as possible. It is a pity that this research is now rather dated as the authors drew a number of interesting inferences from their statistical analysis. Looking at Thai International and Philippine Airlines, for example, 'their number of flight crew per aircraft in 1991 was only about one-third that at Virgin when their average aircraft size was among the largest' and it appeared that flight crews at Thai International provided a significant work input. (Seristo & Vepsalainen, 1997:14).

Consequently, production management and human resource management have to be concerned with work practices. In some ways this is unfortunate for human resource management which has based most of its rationale on the endeavour to express a message of mutual commitment between management and staff. It may, simultaneously, be trying to implement more exacting working conditions, including longer shifts and lower staffing levels, with individuals' work tasks and responsibilities increasing. To some extent, the whole ideology of human resource management may enable its practitioners to sell the greater responsibility as a higher skill level and a more professional commitment (empowerment) but this is a difficult trick to pull off whilst manifestly cutting staff and trying to contain pay. It may lead to accusations from staff of 'slavery at

30,000 feet', a return to the bad old days of 'Fly me, I'm amenable', the notorious sexist slogan on National Airlines, now deceased. (Mackie, 1987) Hochschild (1983), in her study of flight attendants, discussed what she interpreted as an attempt to reduce workers' personalities to a commodity. In short, under competitive conditions, there is no doubt that service workers' ability to perform emotionally becomes the object of rationalization with obvious implications for health and safety. Taking his cue from the emotional labour concept, Wouters (1989) used a survey of KLM staff to criticise Hochschild's work on the grounds that it was rather partial: 'Although the industry speed-ups have shortened the time available for contacts with customers, the range of possible emotion management and of behavioural alternatives had definitely increased.' Nevertheless, one of his respondents made it clear that although the code of conduct had become less hierarchical and less formal, 'easier as this may seem, in fact it is more difficult: correct behaviour may create a distance that is understood as hostile, while a more personal approach may provoke them into trying to use you as a doormat'. (Wouters, 1989:113-114).

The relationship between corporate earnings growth and productivity is not always as clear-cut as Morisot and Seristo claim. BA continued to pursue a policy of cost-cutting in the second half of the 1990s but was not able to compensate for rising fuel costs, a strong pound and increased competition on transatlantic routes. Moreover, the policy was extremely costly in industrial action and staff morale. In their analysis of airline profitability 1986-1991, Oum and Yu (1998) noted similar intervening factors. Korean Air did achieve productivity growth of 53 per cent, galvanized by the entry of Asiana in 1988. However, input costs increased due to strong appreciation of the Korean currency in the period, while the increased competition exerted downward pressure on fares. All Nippon Airways and Cathay Pacific increased productivity by 9 per cent and 14 per cent respectively but profitability fell as a result of input costs rising faster than yields. This was particularly so for Cathay Pacific: a fifty per cent increase in input prices versus a 13 per cent increase in average yields. (Oum & Yu, 1998:236). It may be inferred that a more vigorous attempt by management to contain wage costs and increase productivity by re-negotiating the effort bargain provoked the strike of flight attendants in 1993. In the case of Qantas, the researchers perceived a clear connection between profitability improvement of 23 per cent and 32 per cent productivity growth. Similarly, Singapore Airlines and Thai Airways also improved profitability considerably and again this was attributable to productivity growth of 20 per cent at Singapore Airlines – privatized in 1985 – and no less than 48 per cent productivity growth for Thai Airways.

The contrast between Singapore Airlines and Cathay Pacific is instructive and shows the difference made by good general management, particularly production management. 'SIA is radically better managed than Cathay in every sense of the word, everything from financing to quality of service', according to Ian Wild, airline analyst for SG Securities Asia in Hong Kong. (Westlake & Jayasankaran, 1999:46). As discussed in chapter 6, there are some cost factors beyond the control of an airline's management and for Cathay, the strength of the Hong Kong dollar while other Asian currencies depreciated after 1997 exacerbated its higher costs. Those higher costs looked troublesome long ago and management's belated and clumsy efforts to cut costs have hurt relations with staff. 'The problem should have been addressed earlier in more constructive fashion. It has been a major long-term issue for a long time.' (Westlake & Jayasankaran: 47).

Consequently, about 25 per cent of ground staff jobs were cut in 1998, followed by cuts in cabin staff benefits. As often the case in other airlines, the pilots, faced with cuts in salary and benefits, responded militantly to what they saw as management's arrogant way of demanding compliance. Many called in sick as the deadline for acceptance of the pay deal approached and government mediation was necessary before a settlement was reached. The strong recovery of Cathay Pacific in the first half of 2000, however, suggests that too much emphasis can be placed on cost control. Load factors are more important, to judge by the increase in passenger numbers by 17 per cent and higher loads that resulted in the profit margin leaping from one per cent in 1999 to 13.5 per cent.

By contrast, SIA's load factor (passengers and cargo carried relative to capacity) increased to 75 per cent in the first quarter of 1999 from 70 per cent in the same period in 1998, exemplifying operational efficiency. The Singapore dollar's 20 per cent devaluation against the US dollar gave it a huge recent advantage over Cathay Pacific, while the Singapore government cut mandatory employer pension contributions. Overall, though, it is a learning organization and 'has successfully built up an aviation culture over three decades. This home-grown culture is bred in a flying academy and flight-trianing centres that give Singaporeans the option of making a career with the local airline.' (Jayasankaran,1999:49) From a situation in the 1980s when it had to employ many expatriate pilots, two-thirds of cabin crew, including pilots, are Singaporean, as is the majority of SIA employees, especially in senior management. Perhaps, more importantly, SIA has diversified its markets over the years. Chief Executive Cheong Choong Kong reckoned that this gave 'the flexibility to deploy resources from badly hit regions to the US, Europe and Australia'. (Jayasankaran,1999:49).

Similarly, a further big jump in annual net profit for Qantas of 21 per cent to $182m. in 1997 was attributed by the company's own management to shifting flights away from the depressed Asian market in favour of Europe and North America. But the cost-profitability relationship was well demonstrated by the case of JAL of Japan. A disastrous diversification into the overseas hotel business forced it to write off $1.1bn. in the year to end of March 1998 and use up 30 per cent of its reserves. Without cost-cutting it faced bankruptcy. According to Jeffrey Katz, chief executive of Swissair, 'the operating cost structure is untenable and that is what needs to be fixed. I don't know whether the Japanese infrastructure permits what is required. It's a difficult cultural thing in Japan'. (Landers, 1998:61). Investment analysts agreed that JAL, fully privatized since 1987, needed to lay off high-priced employees and implement drastic salary cuts for those who remain. 'As of November (1998), the average JAL employee made $82,000 a year. That compared with an average of $62,631 for US airlines, according to the Air Transport Association and perks in Japan are still plentiful. JAL flight attendants, for example, receive taxi fares when travelling to and from work.' (Landers,1998). So it is easier said than done to cut costs, as a strike in April 1998 at All Nippon Airways demonstrated. The second Japanese carrier after JAL, ANA was also in financial difficulties, failing to pay a dividend for the first time in 30 years. Yet when the management proposed cuts, the unions called a 15 day strike; the pilots refused to fly selected international routes in protest at salary restructuring that they reckoned amounted to a pay cut of 15 per cent. As with the Cathay Pacific example, a strong recovery in 2000 by JAL showed that revived demand was more important than cost-cutting, although the role of an aggressive restructuring plan could not be discounted.

Another route for management to improve profitability is to increase sales. To enhance yield management, airline operations managers have begun to make fuller use of the enormous volume of reservations data from CRUs and this capability will be increased by development of their own online direct booking facility in cooperation with other airlines. As ever, their yield management techniques ultimately depend upon price discrimination among customers. Price discrimination necessitates physical separation of the market for one type of ticket from those of other tickets, even though the flight journey for all customers for a particular destination at a particular time is the same. From market research, airline managers know that high income travellers, especially business travellers, have relatively price-inelastic demand. They also know that a far bigger segment of customers are very sensitive to prices charged and will shop around for low prices. Hence, to maximize yield management, it is fundamental to prevent the arbitrage that is more common in markets for other products by establishing physical barriers:

'Airlines prevent customers re-selling to each other by making tickets non-transferable. The customer's name is entered on the ticket and, for international travel, proof of identity in the form of a passport needs to be provided at the check-in. It is not possible for customers to buy cheap tickets some time in advance with the intention of selling them to other customers with a more inelastic demand closer to the time of departure.' (Hanlon,1996:157).

The enormous volume of CRS data combined with yield management programs greatly assists the ability of airline production management to forecast the revenue-maximizing seat allocation and their own online booking site will enhance this. The allocation of seats to passengers paying different fares can be made more precise with variation of the number of seats sold at each fare from flight to flight. To some extent, this is already done by the physical separation of seating; we have all seen flight attendants hurriedly drawing the curtain between business and economy class after the first passenger from economy has the temerity to use the business class lavatories. The obvious implication for human resource management is fuller capacity flights, as envisaged by Hochschild. Staff will be called upon to help maintain the separation between business class and economy or APEX fare payers. Often this can create role conflict in customer service and complicate emotional labour.

BA in 1998 decided to focus on profitable point-to-point business and full fare economy traffic. In addition, management decided to introduce the first ever completely flat beds in business class for those prepared to pay the £3300 fare, London to New York. Strategists appeared to be excessively influenced by yield management techniques in their plan to cut capacity by one eighth over three years, mainly by shrinking from Boeing 747s to 777s and from 757s to Airbus 320. The seats lost from the smaller aircraft would be mainly economy seats but 'in reducing size, BA is going against an annual increase of five per cent in air travel which looks set to continue well into the new century'. (Calder, 2000). Furthermore, contestable markets and the entry of low cost carriers on short haul routes make it difficult for the big airlines to carry out the finesse of premium business class fares, so that in the short haul market the additional benefits aimed at the business traveller have become less highly valued. According to Iain Robinson, head of UK corporate travel for American Express, 'travel managers are taking a stronger line on their executives by insisting that they travel in the most economical way possible – be that at the back of the plane or in a no-frills carrier'. (Calder, 2000). Video-conferencing is even less expensive. For the price of a couple of business class jaunts, management can install the most up-to-date system that can render flights over the Atlantic obsolete.

9 Finance and Human Resource Management

The globalization of capital markets has resulted in something of the order of $500 billion of footloose money flowing around the world everyday as electronically transferred funds are used by 24-hour asset managers. As Hazel Henderson has remarked, 'information has become money and money has become information'. (Henderson 1993:34).

As capital can be transferred and relocated with such speed, so institutional barriers in the labour market are broken. BA can carry out an aspect of production management - handling problems or special requirements thrown up by its computerized reservation system - thousands of miles from its UK base. It had a 57-strong team in India to deal with requirements by passengers/customers for vegetarian meals by making logistical arrangements to ensure that the meals are loaded onto the appropriate airplanes. Working shifts, this work team also deciphered and rectified corrupted and inaccurate messages from 20 computerized reservation systems for BA flights booked around the world.

However, an obstacle to an airline contemplating cross-border financial or investment transactions remains the wide divergence in accounting policies and financial disclosure requirements in various countries. Although there is a general tendency towards international harmonization of accounting standards, the substance of airline financial statements often varies significantly from country to country and even between airlines operating within the same country. Therefore, standard-setting authorities are beginning to accept the emergence of global business and the corresponding need for a greater consistency in accounting policies.

As the ability and competitive organizational imperative to rapidly transfer capital and possibly relocate production facilities gouges an ever bigger hole in the internal labour market, dissolving the insulation of human resources from world labour supply, finance becomes a crucial area for human resource management. An understanding of differences in accounting policies and financial disclosure used by international airlines is vital in order to try to avoid incorrect interpretations and conclusions that could adversely affect employees.

Recognizing this problem led to the International Air Transport Association's undertaking a survey of airline accounting practices, in collaboration with KPMG. The report on that survey is extremely useful to those who want to study human resource management in the airline industry. It sets out the critical financial issues according to the chief financial officers of the airlines that participated in the survey. The 'resource' face of human resource management is very well illustrated in this report. Because it is a report on accounting policies, it is free of the ersatz and misleading cults of empowerment and delegation whereby workers have lost trade union and collective bargaining rights in the cause of international competition.

As the report concludes, 'due to poor financial results in the airline industry and competition in the market, airlines are under considerable pressure to reduce costs and improve productivity. With little room for immediate improvement in load factors and little scope to pass unit cost increases on quickly to customers, costs must be reduced in the short term in order to improve profit margins. Airlines find that they must offer substantially the same quality of service in a more efficient manner. As airlines are a service industry, staff related costs are a major expense item. The strong trade unions coupled with the automatic salary adjustments as a result of a continuous rise in the cost of living are threats to many airlines' survival. Several airlines have undertaken staff reduction programmes on a large scale and are now taking steps to increase productivity by means of automation, introduction of more effective work methods and investment in training schemes to enhance efficiency. This is a major focus of financial management's attention. In the case of state-owned airlines, such efficiency programs may be impeded by a moral obligation to keep jobs.' Actually, recent research indicates that, contrary to many policymakers' fears, there may be an increase in airline employment following privatization. (Al-Jazzaf, 1999:45).

Perhaps surprisingly, profitability declines slightly after privatization due to increases in capital investment expenditure and financial and administrative restructuring costs. Less than half the airlines surveyed in the research showed post-privatization improvements in profitability. 'This result supports an earlier claim that short-term profitability after privatization does not necessarily improve since a newly privatized airline spends enormously on expanding and modernizing its fleet and facilities and spending on administrative restructuring. Post-privatization gains in sales and net income surpass the increase in labour force size. The improvement in sales efficiency is found to be statistically significant and shared by almost all the airlines considered in the sample.' (Al-Jazzaf,1999).

The main body of the IATA/KPMAG report is concerned with divergence in accounting practices and financial reporting and with prospects for greater harmonization. It can be used to highlight the relationship with strategic planning that is often claimed to characterize human resource management. Strategy is evidently not static but an approach that develops over time, involving learning through experience, rather than simply the cold application of reason. Firms experiment with different approaches and adapt strategy in the light of circumstances. To the extent that this is so, part of the process of strategy formation must consist of evaluating competitors' moves. To do so, many airlines spend considerable time and effort evaluating and analysing the results of other airlines, though in general, they find it increasingly difficult to compare their results in a meaningful manner with those of other carriers.

One of the most significant inconsistencies in financial reporting is the manner in which aircraft ownership costs are classified in the profit and loss account. Ownership costs have two components: a usage component, and, if the aircraft is financed, a financing component. Depending on whether aircraft are owned or leased under financing or operating leases, the components of ownership costs may be classified differently. The IATA/KPMG report reckons that 'fleet procurement is an integral part of the strategic planning process within the airline industry. The objectives of strategic planning are unique to each airline and influence, to a large extent, the criteria used to determine future fleet requirements'.

The financial structure of an airline may be regarded as rigid if the proportion of fixed to total assets is high. In business generally a substantial amount of working capital is regarded as necessary for financial stability, although no hard and fast rules can be framed to establish this requirement precisely. It is clearly true, however, that in any business, beyond a certain point, investment in fixed assets will reduce the proportion of current assets below the level of safety. In this way even a profitable airline can become insolvent. If its management is tempted to buy from profits more aircraft in times of exceptional demand, when demand slackens it may be left with fixed assets that it cannot use and with insufficient capital to meet current obligations.

This is precisely what happened to several airlines in the years 1990-2 when the Gulf War and recession hit passenger and freight demand. Air

France, Lufthansa and Aer Lingus managements had embarked on 'strategies' that entailed expensive fleet replacement. In 1989 Bernard Attali, the president of Air France, had believed that passenger demand would double in the next 10 years and prospects for freight seemed equally promising; Air France took delivery of 7 new aircraft in 1990. Subsequently, the need to finance losses had been blamed on 'bureaucratic rigidities' with a consequent organisational imperative for 'restrictions'. This may also be true but the problem was undoubtedly exacerbated in each case by grandiose expansionism by business management strategists.

Just before the south east Asian economic crisis of the late 1990s, Philippines Airlines had embarked on a fleet renewal and expansion program. As a result, the management found itself committed to financing costs of US $29million each month in the middle of a recession in what had appeared to be a growth area. By the middle of 1998, management was forced to downsize, provoking a costly dispute with the pilots, leading to 5000 dismissals or lay-offs. After a half-year loss of US $157million, the airline went into protected bankruptcy. The carcass attracted the interest of Northwest, Lufthansa and Cathay Pacific. Financial managers at the latter proposed a 40 per cent stake but, as so often the case, negotiations broke down over the issue of control. (Chin, Hooper & Oum,1999).

Garuda also found itself committed to paying for aircraft that it could not afford. Here a complicating factor was the guarantee given by the Indonesian government for the purchase of 11 Boeing 737s early in 1999. The purchase, costing $62 million dollars annually for eight years, was financed by the U.S. Export-Import Bank. According to people who participated in the negotiations, the guarantee was quietly signed by the Indonesian Finance Minister on the understanding that Garuda would do its best to meet its obligations on its own. Nevertheless, he later asked the government to take on the whole debt, gaining President Habibie's agreement. An official with detailed knowledge of Garuda's accounting reckoned that it obtained the pledge to help fulfil its mandate to link Indonesia's far-flung islands: 'Without those Boeings, the domestic sector would have shrunk, with implications for the economy and for tourism. The government has made it clear that no more guarantees will be provided.' (Murphy, 1999:66).

During the 1980s it was believed that flexibility for financing would be afforded by aircraft leasing. This proved to be an illusion. Undoubtedly leasing can provide flexibility - in the short term. Operating leases, for instance, without exception in the IATA/KPMG survey, are accounted for off balance sheet with lease rentals either expensed as incurred or in equal amounts over the lease term.   Furthermore, many airlines such as Singapore International, elect to sell and lease back certain aircraft as a means of generating cash gain and enhancing fleet flexibility. In common with many airlines, both SIA and Cathay Pacific have used the finance lease system to achieve an effectively lower interest rate by selling their aircraft to companies needing a tax loss. The airlines lease the aircraft back at rates that reflect some of the benefit that the lesson has gained. Cathay has placed finance leases for aircraft in countries where its revenue is strong, linking lease payment to revenue in the same currency as a means of hedging currency fluctuations.   Rather than taking exchange losses against the Hong Kong dollar into its accounts immediately, it defers them until they are realized on settlement of the lease. Until Japanese law restricted it,the company particularly favoured Japan for this type of device.

By contrast, SIA preferred to earn interest on money on deposit, offsetting combined investment earnings against losses. The airline also ran a deferred foreign exchange account over the life of a leased asset to avoid instant foreign exchange losses in any accounting year. As with Cathay Pacific,SIA prefers to lease rather than own aircraft, though both have sometimes and sold aircraft to suit particular circumstances in the used aircraft or financial markets. It should be said, however, that SIA was keen to maintain its reputation for having one of the most modern fleets and embarked on an ambitious expansion programme in 1992.

Accounting for the finance lease method as used by SIA and Cathay Pacific 'is therefore complex and gives rise to more variation amongst the airlines.   Initially, the lessee capitalizes the equipment and records the corresponding lease liability. Several airlines record different values for the asset and the lease liability. The difference is recorded as an increase or reduction in interest expense over some period of time'. (IATA/KPMG Report:10).

Airlines are highly capital intensive and industry-specific financing products are constantly being developed. Leasing is an example of an area where the rigid interpretation of existing accounting standards may lead to financial statements that do not reflect the true substance of transactions. (IATA/KPMG Report:9).

The business of aircraft leasing shows both the strengths and weaknesses of forces making for globalization.   Its mainstay is in circulating or financial capital. During the 1980s, finance capital held sway over industrial capital not so much through dominance by banks as through the monetization of industrial capital.   That is to say that industrial corporations increasingly undertook financial activities, such as credit creation. (Overbeek, 1990:200). They do this by securitization, effecting 'one of the most fundamental changes in the world's financial markets. Securitization is the generic term applied to the process by which financing takes place through the issue of tradeable notes or paper. Debt which has become securitized is thus, in theory at least, more liquid insofar as it may be traded in the market.'(Williams, 1988:132). In the airline business, however, it is not so much individual airline companies that have undertaken financial activities - financially straitened as many have been - but new financial non-bank intermediaries, the aircraft leasing companies. The global airline funding market is a money-making machine, devouring an ever-increasing cash flow to finance its main activities, leasing and trading aircraft. There has been a trend for airlines to lease at least part of their fleets, in line with reducing the rigidity of airline financial structures and focusing on their core activity of producing 'arrivals'. Of the 1,800 aircraft on hire to the world's airlines in 1992, 20 per cent were leased by Guinness Peat Aviation. Set up in 1975 by Tony Ryan, GPA enjoyed spectacular growth. Since 1986 revenue grew by 50 per cent annually, profits by 40 per cent, earnings per share by 30 per cent and dividends by 25 per cent. GPA became increasingly a financial intermediary as financial institutions became reluctant to invest directly in aircraft, completing the first-ever securitization of a package of 14 aircraft in June 1992. According to its chief executive, the demand for finance was way beyond the ability of the airlines. 'We are providing financial solutions to the massive demand for aircraft. We are a significant intermediary between the capital markets and the airlines'. (Cowe, 1992). Yet the planned flotation of $800million of shares in GPA in June 1992 was a failure and had to be aborted.

An article by this book's author in 1993 attempted to provide a case study analysis of GPA. The hypothesis was that only productive capital creates a surplus and this sets limits to the freedom of finance capital to detach itself from actual production. A trend towards monetization is therefore necessarily conjunctural in character. The rise of GPA was conjoined with growth in the airline business. The downturn forced investing institutions to look at the actual performance of the business itself, revealing deficits rather than surpluses in many airlines.GPA had grown very rapidly during the credit boom of the 1980s to a position where it took up 10 per cent of all new orders from the world's manufacturers. It was in a risky business but had a very slender equity base and a very high gearing and needed access to public equity finance. The global offer of

$800 million of shares in GPA in June 1992 was claimed to be the first of its kind. It was such a flop that it might have been the last for some time. The listing was to have been accompanied by a public offer by tender. The global co-ordinator for the issue was Nomura of Japan. Other investment banks engaged for the flotation were Merrill Lynch, Goldman Sachs and Saloman brothers in the USA, with Schroders and BZW covering the UK. Demand from international investors, particularly Swiss, German and Middle Eastern financial institutions, was strong at 13.3m shares. In Ireland and the UK, however, only 7.5m shares were underwritten. Where the flotation was damagingly sandbagged was in the USA, with only 6.5m shares underwritten. Little or no demand from the US financial institutions led to the decision to scupper the entire international share offer. It was significant that the market showing the least enthusiasm for the shares was the USA. Since deregulation, US airlines had been engaged in intermittent price wars, destroying their profitability. Since 1990 they had lost $6.5bn and just before the flotation there was news of yet more trouble about predatory pricing, with smaller airlines bringing anti-trust suits against American Airlines and Delta. American Airlines, the only US airline to make a profit in 1991, disclosed losses for the second quarter of 1992. Hence a wave of stock exchange pessimism assailed aviation-related investment in the USA.

The predicament that GPA found itself in was that financial capital without specific commitment to a physical production process could easily shift itself, on an organized basis, out of an activity that begins to look unprofitable. GPA could not control this process as it was dictated by international investors' view of the profitability of the airline industry. Thus, one could say that if the production of airline arrivals by airlines was not financed directly by the airlines, during a period of recession, then financial capital would detach itself from the business, so setting limits to the ability of third party enterprises, such as leasing companies, to act as intermediaries betwen the two. In the airlines, profitability had slumped since the Gulf war and in the aftermath of deregulation in the big domestic market of the USA, this reduced expectations about GPA's ability to act as an intermediary between capital markets and airlines. The animal spirits - the spontaneous urge to action rather than inaction - of entrepreneurs, such as Tony Ryan, left the financial institutions cold against the background of fierce competition among airlines. Deregulation maay be favoured by the providers of finance capital but this is in contemplation of an ultimate rationalization of the industry, leading to improved profitability. For airline executives, the failure of GPA's flotation was not altogether a bad thing. It would make commercial life just that much harder for weak or small airlines and help towards consolidation in the industry. The corollary was that fares would eventually increase and allow airlines to repair finances and generate surplus revenue again. In such circumstances, financial intermediaries and securitization would come into their own - but not before.

Many airlines have tried a limited measure of employee share ownership, including BA and Iberia. The biggest example remains United. In the early 1990s when the larger US carriers were hit by recession and price cutting, the key to their fortunes was to maintain morale and productivity but cut labour costs. United management tried a different approach in 1994 by handing over 55 per cent of its shares to some groups of employees, in return for concessions on pay. At the time it seemed a desperate stratagem but at least there was an underlying theory; in a service industry afflicted by high labour costs, it might make all the difference if the employees, as well as the shareholders, owned the company. Shareholders could see the logic and 70 per cent voted in favour of the Employee Share Ownership Plan (ESOP). The Clinton government also supported the plan, though the risks for the ordinary employee seemed considerable.

The plan was implemented by the unions' choice of CEO, Gerald Greenwald, who had previously, as Lee Iacocca's deputy, negotiated the federal loan guarantee that saved Chrysler back in the 1980s. Obviously, one big advantage that the scheme might capture was change in the organizational culture towards control by employee commitment, rather than control by rule, a shft one identified as the essence of human resource management. Yet there were complications for United and some of the gilt was soon rubbed off the gingerbread of the scheme. The airline's huge size meant that the scheme had to simultaneously meet the needs of several grades of employees, represented by different unions and paid widely different wage rates. Greenwald tried to mediate among pilots, maintenance workers and non-union workers who accepted pay cuts of between 8 per cent and 16 per cent over a five year period and he would often spend about half his time meeting with United employees and seeking ideas for constructive change – very much like the 'partnership' bargaining promoted by the EU in recent years.

Undoubtedly, the scheme had strengths including that (i) with employee support, the company has cut costs and contained the challenge of low-cost carriers, expanding market share and profits; (ii) having employees more involved in operations management has raised productivity; (iii) the share price tripled, giving the average pilot a $137,000 increment. On the other hand, the share scheme also has weaknesses typical of employee share ownership in that workers often prefer higher or steady wages now, rather than the promise of a big future rise in share price – and these groups often include the lower paid. Such schemes do not necessarily eliminate or even reduce adversarial industrial relations. For example, the flight attendants did not join in the buy-out and it was then difficult to bring them in on terms that they perceived as fair. They form 21,000 members of the Association of Flight Attendants that represents 40,000 flight attendants at 26 airlines and first utilized its notorious CHAOS ('create havoc around our system') tactics in 1993 in a dispute with Alaska Airlines. Human resource management attempts to exclude from its lexicon any encouragement to activities such as collective bargaining and certainly pattern bargaining by reference to leading pay settlements and comparison with the earnings of other employee groups. Nevertheless, there are plausible theories of motivation, such as equity theory, that insist that such comparisons are part of the picture. No matter how much management attempts to charm them away by piping its Pied Piper tunes of empowerment, they also risk losing their employee children who hear the tune more jarringly. Their disgruntlement does not always manifest itself as formal grievances – indeed it may be irrational to do so in a punitive climate. Hence it was recently reported on the internet – in response to a request for good or bad experiences with cabin crew – that service on one United flight Melbourne to Los Angeles was unsatisfactory. 'We had a full flight minimum service strike; something to do with staff share allocation. Also we had a three hour in-flight dissertation from one flight attendant regarding how bad United was to work for, how the pilots copped a sweet deal but the attendants were badly done by.'

The close connection of finance and human resource management is well brought out by the curious episode that involved BA's consulting subsidiary, Speedwing, taking over the human resource and production management functions at Olympic, the Greek state carrier. What looked to be a simple financial contract led to a dispute about Speedwing's handling of finances and the accountability of the management team. Human resource management must ultimately include the pursestrings and Olympic's deteriorating financial position necessitated drastic organizational changes. Hence BA declined to take up its option to buy 20 per cent of Olympic and the finance ministry, Olympic's only shareholder, ended the contract.

A final financial factor that strongly affects human resource management is employee pensions.   The KPMG report noted that significant and differences exist throughout the world in practices relating to employee persons and accounting for pensions.   One fundamental difference is the level of pension benefits provided by pension schemes sponsored by governments.   A complication in the restructuring of Lufthansa preparatory to privatization, was the need to remove employees from the state-administered pension scheme at a cost - to the state - of around DM 1.5 billion.   OTV, the main public service union, insisted that the timetable for the privatization rights issue could be met only if the Lufthansa board set out all the new pension arrangements in a binding collective agreement.

Pre-privatization and post-privatization pension schemes have also affected the finances of BA.   As might be expected, the old scheme is fully funded, had been in surplus for 10 years, and, BA is obliged to guarantee benefits at all times.   The new scheme is in deficit.   Hence, in 1999 the company tried to merge the pension funds and then take a pensions contributions 'holiday'.   Although the merger was approved by trustees of both schemes, critics alleged a conflict of interests as BA's finance director was chairman of both boards of trustees.   Opposition to the pensions scheme merger, led by Mike Post, a retired BA pilot, outpointed BA's management with only 22 per cent of BA's pensioners voting in favour of the plan in a ballot in which 62 per cent voted. (Harrison, 1999).

In a peculiar instance of 'punter capitalism' (defined as popular capitalism with widespread buying and selling and the emphasis on short term profitability and high share prices), there was a rush of premature retirements among American Airlines pilots in 1998.   The sudden exodus depleted employee numbers so much that American operations management was forced to curtail its schedules.   Under US aviation regulations, the retirement age for commercial pilots is 60. American, with 9,000 pilots, can normally expect to lose 20 captains to retirement and replace them with new recruits.   Under the company's retirement plan, benefits for pilots were derived from a pooled mutual fund.   Its value had fallen ten per cent and, under fund rules, pilots had a three month period in which to make withdrawals.   Hence benefits in September 1998 were set at share prices as they were in July when the market was far higher.   In the words of American's chief pilot and vice-president: 'The money managers are telling us that if you have to retire prior to the end of the first quarter of next year, you have got to go now.   We have had a lot of guys go out early just because of the market.' (Usborne, 1998).   In response, American showed human resource management flexibility by ordering pilots who had been promoted to general management to return to flying more or less full time.

This chapter and the previous chapter show that finance and production management are the drivers of the 'hard' approach to human resource management. Clearly cost drivers and financial information is useful in evaluating the performance of the airline industry. However, the reverse of this coin is also possible, *i.e.* that non-financial information is useful in evaluating financial performance in the industry. To consider this, Riley (1999) correlated the customer service performance of US domestic airlines with their financial performance, relating expenses to revenues and to customer complaints. He concluded that non-financial performance information helps predict quarterly rvenue, expenses and operating income. Such performance measures are to do with co-operativeness, team spirit and morale.

It is highly significant that the IATA/KPMG report stated that 'one of the principal challenges currently facing airline management is to achieve direct labour participation in the financial results of companies. It is the task of management to convince airline union leadership and rank and file that their success is directly dependent on their contribution to productivity and efficiency and is critical to survival'. The statement reflects the dichotomy between the 'resource' and 'human' aspects that sum up the issues in the debate about human resource management. It was because personnel management was adjudged not to have delivered the necessary participation of employees in corporate strategies, in order to continually enhance performance, that human resource management was fashioned. However, though clearly more than a passing fad, it is far from being generally acceptable among airline employees. The reasons for this and problems that will continue to call for personnel management as the 'human' aspect of human resource management are discussed in the final chapter.

10 Personnel Management

Of course, it will seem illogical to have a chapter entitled 'personnel management' in a book about human resource management. After all, human resource management developed partly as a result of the alleged failures of personnel management to deliver improved performance. (Skinner, 1979). In practice, however, although there had been a constitutional change in employee relations such that collective bargaining procedures have been diminished to a considerable extent with the advent of the ostensibly more individually-based human resource management, the transformation to a fully-fledged new approach to management had been far more limited (Sisson & Storey, 1990).

There have been moves towards human resource management in the international airline business. They largely reflected just such a switch from the collective aspect of employment management to the individual. This has emanated from the hostile, intensely competitive environment of an industry suffering from considerable over-capacity as the anticipated long-haul growth did not materialise, whereas the growth occurred among smaller, no-frills companies operating short-haul services. It has been the 'resources' aspect of human resource management that has been emphasised, to the detriment of the 'human' aspect. In this final chapter, the main issues in this dichotomy will be reviewed. In addition, however, the chapter will cover other personnel issues that will always be personnel issues - under whatever title - that have not yet been discussed, such as training and health and safety.

'Resources' and 'Human' Aspects

Two key texts that encapsulate this still unresolved problem for human resource management are Arlie Hochschild's 'The Managed Heart' and Jan Carlzon's 'Moments of Truth'. A moment of truth is the moment in time when a customer first comes into contact with the people, systems, procedures and products of an organization and which leads to the customer's making a judgement about the quality of the organization's services. From this follow many of the organizational changes that have become associated with human resource management. 'Flattening the pyramid is the process that Carlzon implemented at Scandinavian Airlines System (SAS), whereby authority was delegated downwards towards those dealing with the customers. Carlzon pointed out that hierarchies create a situation where those higher up the organization feel that they can justify their role only by issuing instructions, setting controls and carefully monitoring behaviour. Such actions make those responsible to them reluctant to use their initiative and this in turn leads to dissatisfaction amongst those customers who require some non-routine response from their organization.' (Blois, 1992). A subsequent study of how SAS tried to develop the quality of its service based on a genuine understanding of customers' true needs, identified no less than 40 customer needs and concerns, suggesting some practical problems with implementation of a 'policy' as such. (Gustafsson, Ekdahl & Edvardsson,1999).

Clearly, such efforts go hand-in-hand with the idea of human resource management as signifying a shift from control to commitment. (Walton, 1985) Jon Clark (1993) later commented that it would be more apt to talk of moving from compliance with works rules to enthusiastic commitment or identification with organisational aims, although the fuller interpretation of the Harvard approach to human resource management is that it entails mutual commitment of company (senior management) and workers. Clark was nonetheless administering a healthy corrective to the tendency elsewhere to diminish the importance of rules and procedures, due process in short, as a bureaucratic obstruction.

It may be argued that in some circumstances this is justified. It is never justified - otherwise management becomes arbitrary, opening the way to favouritism and jobbery. In 1989 BA dismissed a stewardess for allegedly selling champagne for club class to economy class customers and pocketing the proceeds.   At first, the director of operations expressed absolute confidence that the decision taken, after two appeals and a final day-and-a-half hearing, was correct. However, her union, the TGWU, took strike action. Also, those representing her drew BA's attention to several similar cases where staff involved had not been dismissed. The director of operations then decided that the differential treatment had not been justifiable as a matter of good management practice. Senior management now felt able to take the opportunity to assert a firmer line on discipline. He noted that it has been said that certain conduct in relation to the taking of drink and food from aircraft is acceptable as part of the custom and practice of the company; whatever may have been practised in the past would not be tolerated from now on. Nevertheless, the case illustrates the importance of disciplinary procedures because settlement - BA offered reinstatement - was reached as the industrial tribunal hearing was about to begin.

Bureaucracy has frequently been a scapegoat in the airline business. Air France senior management was still blaming bureaucratic structures at the time of the 1994 revised restructuring plan and fresh injection of state funding.   Before the 1991 strategic plan, CAP93, Arthur Andersen consultants had identified bureaucratic structures as a contributant to moderate competitive performance. Industrial action among cabin crew at BA in 1997 was preceded by statements from senior management to the effect that the company was still characterized by some of the trappings of nationalized industry and was not as efficient or competitive as it should be.

Elsewhere, down-sizing moves have been tougher and accompanied or followed by attempts at managed culture change towards empowerment - with enpowerment meaning engineering a situation of voluntary acceptance of more exacting work practices and individual responsibility for quality and errors. As workers' countervailing power evaporates, so will the need for management ideology to be so sophisticated.

From this perspective, approaches such as 'Moments of Truth' appear more tactical than strategic. They do not empower but set the employee in a position of ceaseless activity on behalf of the company and, of course, monitored to do so, not only by customers but by colleagues. Arlie Hochschild has written the definitive work on this in her study of the exploitation of the emotional labour of flight attendants. Her point is that, although coping with passenger stress and anxiety has always been a part of the flight attendants skill, Total Quality Management has de-skilled by making the attendant's 'learn to act'. The lessons in deep-acting – acting 'as if the cabin was your home' and 'as if this unruly passenger has a traumatic past' - are themselves a new development in employee training. The mind of the emotion worker, the source of the ideas about what mental moves are needed to settle down an irate passenger, has moved upstairs in the hierarchy so that the worker is restricted to implementing standard procedures. This is not to say that the standard procedures are easy ; on the contrary a lot of discretion is required in dealing with customers. However, as this job role is primarily carried out by women, management expect them to be particularly skilled at 'naturally' exercising this work autonomy – in developing a rapport with passengers, responding to emergencies, coping with sick, nervous or intoxicated passengers and using appropriate body language, trainees are often told that 'basically, you just have to use your common sense'. (Taylor & Tyler, 2000:87). This detracts from the fact that the sensitivity required is not 'common' and devalues the skills required.

The overall definition of the task is more rigid than it once was, according to Hochschild, and the worker's field of choice about what do do is greatly narrowed. A new executive in Virgin was surprised at just how hard flight attendants have to work: 'The job was a cross between a barman and a lavatory attendant – loos and booze, as he later described it, recalling with particular distaste, the Sisyphean task of keeping the outdated toilets presentable for eight hours at a stretch'. (Jackson, 1995:150). Within the boundaries of the job, more and more actual sub-tasks are specified. Did the flight attendant hand out magazines? How many times? How were the magazines handed out? With a smile? With a sincere smile?

Hochschild cites the examples of SIA's advertising the glamorized cabin hostess as 'the Singapore Girl'. To convey the idea of in-flight pleasure with a lyrical quality, most SIA advertisements were essentially large, soft-focus colour photographs of various hostesses - as were those of several other airlines.

The selection procedure of SIA exemplifies the effect of such market-oriented strategies as human resource management. The girls must be between 18 and 25, fluent in English, slim and attractive with a clear complexion, taller than 1.58 metres, with a pleasant personality and a smile. An increasing number of graduates apply.

Fifty girls are selected from the first interview - 'first impression impact' - where the criteria are eloquence, beauty and communicability. The second interview involves updated psychometric tests. By this stage, the batch (as the airline terms them) of putative hostesses will be reduced to 20. The final stage of the selection procedure is tea and biscuits with the company's directors. The (predominantly male) directors give the girls the once over and, if they take their fancy, they are hired. Apart from some managers, no other employees meet the directors.

Although no one would admit it, the training was implicitly sexual: the Singapore Girl's brief was to be irresistible to Western and Japanese men. They are also taught to shake hands with a firm grip - 'how businessmen like it'. They are also told to read up on world affairs so that they know something about most passengers' professions. It would be extremely and perversely 'politically correct' for us not to perceive the attractions in all this from the viewpoint of the employees themselves. One chief stewardess reported that the training course changed her life. As well as being more confident, better groomed and more poised, she now had a smile and knew how to use it. 'They don't want us to put on an artificial smile, so they train to smile with sincerity. It brightens up your whole face.' (Bellos, 1989).

A study by Tyler and Abbott (1998:433-442) tended to support the stance of Hochschild. Just as she had concentrated on emotional 'labour, they theorized that the

> body work that flight attendants must undertake has to be concealed to the extent that, the better women are at its performance, the more invisible it becomes. To secure employment as a flight attendant, a woman must achieve and maintain a particular state of embodiment, prescribed primarily according to an instrumentally imposed concept of a feminine aesthetic and practised largely according to constraint, containment and concealment. This body work must be undertaken in addition to physically demanding manual labour, as well as the emotional and sexual labour which flight attendants are required to perform. Female flight attendants were found to be selected for being able to perform aesthetically without making the end result seem like a performance, that is without revealing that the performance itself requires labour.

In the previous edition of this book it was suggested that there was no necessary link with business strategy here. Such customer-oriented policies merely have 'the result that contact personnel know little more than that they should be nice to customers (smile a lot, make eye contact with the customer- though not, of course, in a challenging way)' (Blois, 1992). However, the Tyler and Abbott study shows that the management strategies deployed in the airline industry do involve the habitual maintenance of the body as a form of work discipline. They further suggested that employees who are deficient in any such respect can be encouraged to work harder by way of compensating the airline that employs them for what they come to perceive as their own failure. Some of the flight attendants that they interviewed suggested that airlines deliberately recruited those who did not match up to the aesthetic ideals that are depicted in advertisements in order to encourage workers to make up for their perceived deficiency by being nicer, working harder, smiling more sweetly and so on.

Occupational psychologists have been employed in various businesses, getting people to learn to 'act' on the jobs. Drawing on Stanislavski, they distinguish two types of occupational acting: 'Surface' acting, whereby the worker simply puts on an outward appearance - as in

'How are we today, sir?' and 'deep' acting, whereby the emotional labourer internalises the correct feeling for the job. Singapore Girl could be doing either of these - but when she stops smiling, you will know that she is on emotional labour strike. That is an unlikely eventuality, however. There would appear to exist in SIA's personnel management the fundamental procedural norms that signify commitment-based human resource management. It is a learning organization and has successfully developed an aviation culture over the last two decades. 'SIA trains harder. For example, its stewardesses – the iconic Singapore Girls – are trained over four months while Western airlines settle for for two.' (Jayasankaran,1999:49).

By contrast, where there seems to be less attention to long term development in the procedural norms of personnel management, there is more likely to be overt conflict. In 1993 the elegant flight attendants of Cathay Pacific temporarily revived Hong Kong's somnambulant trade union movement when they went on strike. Here the glamorized emotional part of the job rebounded in management's face when a cost-cutting exercise required flight attendants to do more menial jobs. Cost-cutting may have been necessary but insufficient management thought had gone into it. After the strike was settled there were allegations of victimization as some staff were dismissed and rancour continued through the 1990s as gauche attempts to cut costs harmed staff relations.

What has happened to flight attendants as human resource management has been utilized as a marketing tool illustrates the widespread devaluation of the word 'professional'. For companies, a 'professional' flight attendant is one who has completely accepted the rules of standardization. The flight attendant who most nearly meets the appearance code ideal is therefore 'the most professional' in this regard:

> The image of Virgin Atlantic is reflected in our cabin crew who must be friendly and approachable when accommodating the varying needs of our passengers. It is a responsible job and involves everything from the anticipation and understanding of each customer's needs, providing the highest possible standard of comfort and customer care, to the safety and security of our passengers and aircraft.
>
> You must remember you are the face of the airline. Even after a long and tiring flight, grooming must be immaculate. Special training will be given in hair styling, skincare and make-up so you can compliment our outstanding uniform. (Recruitment folder, Virgin Atlantic, 1999)

This potential tension between intensified labour and job satisfaction seems to be inherent in human resource management generally. It is, however, virtually certain to be manifested in the airline business which trades on imagery of the exotic and the pleasurable. From the western perspective, the evidence seems considerable that permitting the primacy of the market to intrude into human resource management by non-negotiated decisions will reduce employee welfare.

Supervisors

In Hochschild's study of Delta Airlines, supervisors did more than oversee workers. At this point in Delta's history, the fear hierarchy was bending and supervisors had to pose as big sisters in the Delta family - bigger but not by much. These largely female, immobile and non-unionized workers are not greatly feared by their underlings, nor much envied, as the comment of one flight attendant suggests:

> It's not a job people want very much. Some girls go into it and then bounce rightback on the line. The pay is an inch better and the hours are a whole lot worse. And you have to talk oatmeal. My supervisor called me into her office the other day. I've used seven out of twenty-one days of available sick leave. She says, 'I don't want to have to tell you this. It's what I *have* to tell you. You've used up too much of your sick leave.' She has to take it from her boss and then take it from me - from both ends. What kind of job is that?

According to Hochschild, supervisors monitor the supply of emotional labour. They patch leaks and report breakdowns to the company. They must also cope with the frustrations that workers suppress while on the job. As one Delta base manager explained - 'I tell my supervisors to let the girls ventilate. It's very important that they get that out. Otherwise, they'll take it out on the passengers.' So, Hochschild reasons, the supervisor who grades the flight attendant on maintaining a 'positive' and 'professional' attitude is also exposed to its underside.... Managing someone else's formerly managed frustration and anger is itself emotional labour.

Managerial surveillance at the supervisory level appears to have increased in respect of the bodily presentation expected in emotional labour and customer care. An example of such supervision in relation to surface acting was the enforcement of Uniform and Grooming regulations at two airlines. 'Flight attendants were under the line management of a Standards Development Officer (SDO) who was responsible for checking and monitoring the appearance of flight attendants through spot checks and pre-flight grooming checks.' (Taylor & Tyler, 2000:87). These SDOs, responsible for enforcement of the companies' uniform and behaviour regulations, were also senior flight attendants and part of the cabin crew, themselves supervised and appraised by senior management, often by way of the 'mystery shopper' technique on certain flights.

Training

The stance taken by management on training and development is a useful yardstick for judging the quality of human resource management in a company. Short-termism and little attention to development of the employees, or worse still, extensive sub-contracting of tasks and part-time staffing, indicates a 'hard' or resource-centred policy. Human resource accounting and the time period chosen for the balance sheet will play a part in this. Although it is difficult to generalize about training across the range of occupations in an airline company, the SIA example demonstrates that training costs depend to a considerable extent on the aims and success of staff selection procedures. An airline can aim to select skilled staff requiring the minimum of training – or its management can aim to select staff with limited skills (but high potential) and be prepared to invest in substantial training. Using the human resource development strategy, the airline might expect to recoup all or part of the difference in pay between skilled and unskilled workers. The need for regular human resource audits to determine clear aims at the selection stage is obvious; otherwise selection and training efforts will be contradictory.

Training of pilots is clearly expensive and runs into tens of thousands of pounds. Again, human resource planning is essential in order for management to be aware of bulges in recruitment needs. Airline pilot training schools in the USA were advertising in 2000 that the major airlines would lose a significant number of their pilots by the year 2002 due to retirement, so it was opportune to become professionally trained as an airline pilot. Such schools offer fairly competitive courses in terms of fees and it is a fact that many young people have gone to the USA to train there. However, even though it is much cheaper, the licence that is issued on qualifying is a Federal Aviation Administration licence and not recognized as a full CPL (Commercial Pilots Licence) in the UK or several other countries. In the past, European aviation systems had diverged in their requirements. In line with EU regulation 3922/91 on harmonization of technical requirements, member states of the Joint Aviation Authorities (JAA) undertook to develop Joint Aviation Requirements (JARS). These include the fields of certification, aircraft maintenance, aircraft operations and flight crew licensing. JAR-FCL is the code adopted for flight crew licensing and has been developed for all categories of pilot licences to permit use of licences and ratings without further formality in participating states.

The incentive for taking a course in the USA and gaining an American licence is that six flying certificates may be obtained: private pilot licence; commercial pilot licence; instrument rating; multi-engine rating; certified flight instructor instrument, and, certified flight instructor. This means that they are enabled to obtain a job as an instructor and thereby build up their hours towards 700 – the minimum required for a CPL in the UK. They would be required to convert to a UK licence in order to work professionally in the UK. Such a conversion would require negotiation with the Civil Aviation Authority but it is proposed that an FAA PPL holder with more than 75 hours flying experience would need to take JAR-FCL examinations in Aviation Law and Human Performance, demonstrate a knowledge of JAA requirements and pass the PPL skill test.

It was reported in April 2000 that in one of the examinations for JAR-FCL ambiguities of language produced questions described as 'close to gobbledegook'. At the Oxford Aviation School, regarded as one of the leading air training establishments in the world, all 30 trainees failed, whereas at least 90 per cent would usually pass before joining BA, Aer Lingus or other airlines. Twenty nine countries contributed aspects of the examination, devised by the Joint Aviation Authority, to gain a European Airline Transport Pilot's Licence. 'Each country's input was translated into the various languages and fed into a computer but its memory bank became a kind of tower of Babel where the intricate details became lost in babble.' (Tory, 2000). There are always initial problems with harmonization and the chief instructor at Oxford was reportedly optimistic: 'It has been a problem but we are upbeat. After all, licences will be valid for employment throughout Europe.'

A potentially more serious issue of pilot examination malpractice, rather than ambiguous questions, was alleged by South African Airways to the Civil Aviation Authority of South Africa in March 2000. The CAA received an affidavit from a former airline pilot alleging that 8 pilots had been involved in a scheme to fraudulently pass their Airline Transport Pilot written examinations. Initial investigations proved inconclusive but the CAA decided to appoint an independent review panel.

A big difference in pilot recruitment could be made by training more female pilots. BA doubled the number of its female pilots between 1998 and 2000, Ruth Smith becoming the airline's 100th female pilot when she gained her UK Commercial Pilots Licence at Oxford Air Training School and commenced flying Boeing 737s from Gatwick. Globally, female pilots now have their own representative organization, ISA, the International Society of Women Airline Pilots. Founded in 1978 by 21 women pilots from various airlines, the society had grown to 560 members from 96 airlines in 36 countries by 2000. The ISA's mission is to encourage women to enter the airline pilot workforce as active cockpit crew via education. It seeks to promote aviation science among women and provide education for all airlines and all pilots. The organization offers some scholarships for pilot training. A survey on sexual harassment undertaken by ISA indicated that airline managements could do more to counteract it in their training of male crew members

Globalization must nowadays be a significant feature of training programs. In an attitude survey of pilots from the USA, the Philipines and Taiwan, along with flight attendants from the USA, Hong Kong, Japan, Korea, Thailand, Singapore and Taiwan, the respondents completed a questionnaire about group processes on the flight deck. The research was modelled on Hofstede's well-known study that identified four dimensions of cultural variation in work values, such as individualism and power distance. One dimension revealed by the flight deck survey reflected high power distance and collectivism and applied primarily to the 8 Asian groups. The second dimension, reflecting individualism and moderate power distance, was used by the US flight attendants. The third dimension, reflecting individualism and low power distance, was used almost exclusively by the US pilots. The researchers concluded that the ideal training program will be designed in conjunction with members of the appropriate culture and that training will be successful only if it can resonate with national culture as globalization meant that efforts were needed to understand differences in national culture. (Merritt & Helmreich,1996).

A crucial question affecting training policy is how elaborately organized is the company. Elaborately organized companies (those that do most of their work in-house and sub-contract relatively little) employ people on tasks requiring the exercise of a wide variety of skills. Airlines in particular require a mix of technical and human skills and the problem of integrating them must be considered when setting out any syllabus for training. These remarks apply mainly to ground staff. A huge contradiction has developed alongside Total Quality Management programs in that they have often accompanied cuts in permanent staff to control head count with more tasks being sub-contracted or done by part-time staff. In the case of one major airline at the start of its big labour-cutting exercise, it was evident that training for all front-line staff had declined woefully in the previous few years. (Harper, 1999). The brusque attitude of some check-in staff is probably not their fault but that of poor training standards. Many are part-timers who have been taught the basics and no more. The worst tend to be employed by handling agencies as opposed to those employed directly by the airline. The industry cannot keep up with the rollover of staff in jobs now perceived as insecure and training is kept to the minimum, a vicious circle of low human resource development that imposes costs.

The results of inadequate training are reflected in revenues and costs. Losses are difficult to identify but TQM programs have directed attention at prevention rather than cure. Nevertheless, there is still a tendency to gloss over them as inevitable costs of production, a tendency exacerbated by sub-contracting repairs to baggage damaged in transit. Some recovery can be made from episodes of baggage wrongly routed by computer system failures if staff can be well trained in speedily compensating customers. This is an age of league tables and we are so accustomed to comparisons of one airline against others in the press that we tend to overlook the fact that, *pace* benchmarking, this way of measuring efficiency is not very useful for other than competitive activities – such as gaining market share. Maybe this is a latent function of human resource management– to condition us as consumers to measuring all kinds of work performance by comparison, hardly a human characteristic.

Inadequate training may hinder an airline from meeting all the demand for its services or reduce demand by reducing quality. Small wonder that managements have been enthusiastic for TQM – almost every member of staff can affect the image of the services offered to customers. Looking at costs, inadequate training can prevent an airline from optimizing use of equipment and plant. Incorrectly used equipment may fail to produce needed changes in operations or requires an excessive proportion of staff to equipment. Finally, if the much-vaunted integration feature of human resource management is to mean anything, it ought to be concerned if inadequate training increases the cost of recruitment and remuneration. Inflated recruitment costs and inflated salaries are frequently caused by competitive bidding for trained personnel as a result of an airline's inability to train effectively.

Negotiated Team Working

It is essential not to be totally negative about human resource management. It does contain a powerful ideological message that can simply reinforce managerial prerogative in cost control, culminating in restoration of treatment of labour as a mere factor of production. However, this is short-sighted and very much short term. We cannot overlook the fact that due attention to the human aspect and preservation of the collective due process in industrial relations can produce integrative bargaining and shared gains- but this is an arduous aspiration demanding as much perseverance as old-style productivity bargaining. It cannot simply be imposed and then 'sold' as 'commitment'.

In 1989 KLM Cargo was in various financial difficulty, such that the board in Schipol was considering closure of the London Heathrow organisation. It had been making a loss for some years and, despite a £6 million investment in the facility, had been unable to approach profitability. There was a palpable lack of cohesion between management and staff, every change that management attempted being met by instant rejection. There was a deep distrust of management motives and an acute lack of accountability on the part of staff. The operation ran continuously but work patterns were such that employees did not work with the same colleagues or supervisors for more than 3 or 4 consecutive shifts. Tracing the source of any problem was difficult as it was always a story of 'the other staff'. Assessment of staff was a nightmare because no supervisor worked with an individual for long enough to build up an accurate picture of his or her capabilities. Career development and training were also affected; there was an implicit 'don't care' attitude and the staff did not feel part of the organization and had no goal to work towards.

The management had heard about the Japanese concept of team working and visited Nissan at Sunderland to see it in action. They took copious notes and sought advice, following which they began to introduce team working. There was plenty of scepticism. The crucial part of the whole process was selecting the composition of the teams. To do this effectively a working party of staff, employee representatives and management, was set up. This group to ascertain specific problems

consulted all members of staff. Eventually, the teams were formed and -
for the first 3 months, while the teams were settling down, a 'transfer post'
was established. Every team and its leader went away for a 2 day training
session and the work patterns were altered to ensure that the teams did
work together - no easy task in view of spasmodic coverage required to
service all flights. The whole process was staggered to enable any teething
problems to be ironed out before another area was tackled.

After five years, team working had been introduced throughout. For
complete coverage there were 5 work patterns and broadly 5 teams. The
team concept was so successful that the office and warehouse teams for
each work pattern combined to form one larger team so that its members
could appreciate the problems encountered by their colleagues in other
areas. Each team had its own performance targets to aim at and the team
leaders would report on the teams' achievements at a monthly meeting with
production management.

Team working helped the organization achieve a reported 22 per cent
increase in productivity, a 30 per cent decrease in overtime, while
throughput increased by 20 per cent. By the end of the financial year
1993/94, KLM Cargo made profits of half a million pounds. The results
were undeniable with the teams bonding so strongly that they began to
organize regular social events.

The point is that this change involved consultation and negotiation.
KLM maintained consultation and negotiation within its corporate culture.
Den Hartog, deputy president of KLM, accepted that fundamental issues
require three way negotiations. Within the management team, senior vice-
president for personnel and organization conducts negotiations with the
seven unions and employee organizations. The main statutory
(Netherlands law) joint staff council at Schipol also regularly attends to
union issues, though only where terms of employment and organizational
issues converge. 'We must remember that the move to a flexible
organization will be gradual. We are on the right track and not nearly as
inflexible as some of us think. Besides that, the need for flexibility offers
new opportunities, such as part-time working, that the joint staff council
has been pushing for some time. Careful negotiating has already produced
good results for cabin attendants but I fully realise that it will not be so easy
to achieve in other departments.' (KLM Staff Magazine, 1992).

This example is local but for all functions pertaining to human
resource management, people need to share information. For rapid
checking of problems and critical maintenance decisions, teamworking
may require networks on a global scale, inside and outside the organization.

Participation

KLM senior management did not believe that the idea of direct labour participation through an equity stake in the company was a practicable strategy. How factors such as capital expenditure were conducted would be problematic. All the same, Den Hartog, deputy president, was on record as saying 'we are certainly on the look-out for ways and means of increasing the interest of the personnel in KLM as an enterprise operating on the open capital market. Though we are not, in the first instance, giving personnel a greater say in company affairs, nor is there any chance that real influence on policy by KLMers through, say, the joint staff council, is going to be put on the agenda. Let's be quite clear about that. So it looks as though the company buy-out is a peculiarity of the American fiercely deregulated market' (KLM Staff Magazine, 1992).

The main examples of such financial participation are United (60 per cent), TWA (45 per cent) and North West (35 per cent). TWA's mission statement, it may be noted from the industrial relations perspective, is specifically about rules: 'No longer are workers hired to follow the rules; we want people who will make their own rules. Under the old way, you waited for instructions; under the new way you will aggressively take actions that will improve our service - making it more efficient and more valued from our customers' standpoint.' It has long been known that, notwithstanding its merits, employee share allocation can also be troublesome. A full in-flight minimum service 'strike' or work-to-rule by flight attendants took place on some United routes in 1999 as a result of discontent over share allocation. Nor will share allocation *per se* enable financially weak airlines to overcome their difficulties. Labour relations difficulties at Philippines Airlines were alleviated by a series of collective agreements in which employees showed their faith by investing nearly half a million pounds in a stock option plan to become part-owners but macro-economic weaknesses were intractable.

Share allocation is one form of participation but it may also be done by means of works councils, as is the case in several western European countries. Lufthansa and KLM operate such representative bodies, while Air France has the slightly different comité d'entreprise. In 1994, the Council of Ministers of the EU issued a council directive on the establishment of European works councils for informing and consulting employees. This measure applies to all companies with more than 1,000 EU employees and at least 150 in more than one member state and consequently applies to all major airlines.

Equal opportunities is a vital area of personnel management that can benefit from increased participation but, more particularly, from observance of procedures and due process. In one unfair dismissal case, a female airline pilot, the only woman among Airtours 178 pilots, claimed that she had been subjected to a relentless onslaught of sexual harassment and discrimination that led to her dismissal. It was alleged that a false and biased report by a senior pilot led to her failing a twice yearly piloting check. She was then called to a disciplinary hearing and dismissed. Despite complaints to senior officers and other high ranking personnel, nothing was done and she had become too afraid to complain.

The International Society of Women Airline Pilots (ISA) has carried out surveys of sexual harassment through 134 of its members.

> Despite the media attention usually concentrated on sexual harassment, the ISA participants reported total gender discrimination incidents as both more frequent and more significant. Of the significant incidents reported, 55 per cent (37 incidents) were categorized as gender discrimination and 45 per cent as sexually oriented harassment. (Wentworth, 1995)

The ISA points out that airlines recognize the importance of Crew Resource Management (CRM) training that emphasizes effective communication in the cockpit on technical and procedural aspects of flights. Sexual harassment is rightly difficult to prove legally but interpersonal conflicts of this kind can be detract from flight safety. ISA issues advice to members about how to handle 'challenging' situations involving gender discrimination and sexual harassment in the airline industry. (Quoted with permission by ISA +21).

Unions that represent ground staff also issue such advice more generally among their more widespread membership. In August 1999, a single mother who could not look after her baby properly because she was asked to work 16 hour shifts at Heathrow airport won her claim for unfair dismissal due to sex discrimination against South African Airways. The industrial tribunal found that Annette Cowley, a cargo officer, had been unfairly dismissed after complaining about her hours of work, ordered the airline to pay her three years salary and criticised its 'wholly unreasonable demands'. (Verkaik, 1999).

Health and Safety

In most general discussions and diagnoses of whether human resource management is less reality than rhetoric, training programmes that indicate a long term, investment in their human capital by corporate senior managers are often taken as an acid test. In airlines, this is less appropriate. For flying crews, training is considerable and has to be. However, even here, as has been noted, there is a tendency to employ appearance rather than experience among flight attendants, a practice accentuated in the USA by the 2 tier salary.

Health and safety considerations mean that training must be taken much more seriously by airlines compared with other businesses. But this is no guarantee against short cuts. Health and safety is not insulated against costs. Improved training of pilots, particularly in emergency situations, is needed. However, several changes in the industry are likely to put more, rather than less pressure on pilots. Many newer aircraft such as Boeings 757, 767 and 747-400 and the Airbus 320 have only 2 rather than 3, crew on the flight deck. Negotiations to standardize pilots' hours in the European Union countries may result in longer hours. The British Airline Pilots' Association warned that rules easing restrictions on flight crews working hours could increase risk of accidents. General secretary, Chris Darke pointed out that pilot or crew error is the biggest single cause of international air accidents. 'Regulations in Britain have been progressively tightened but the new regulations mean that crews will be working harder and will be on duty for more landings and take-offs. You cannot treat pilot fatigue in this cavalier fashion without suffering the consequences.' (Smithers,1995).

Safety factors vary considerably in different parts of the world. Europeans are trying to maintain or improve working conditions, while Africans and South Americans are fighting to secure for their flight crews and pilots basic standards that have been accepted as the norm in western countries. At the 1996 conference of the International Federation of Airline Pilots, worries were raised about safety and stress amid growing pressure from employers to adopt new work practices. There were problems of aircraft and crew being hired from foreign sources in that several countries were somewhat lax complying with standards set by the International Civil Aviation Transport Association.

Blame is otherwise often attributed to the aircraft, particularly older aircraft; the airline cargo sector in general has a reputation for pressing elderly aircraft into service. Nevertheless, the big Boeing twins are relatively safe, as proved by millions of safe hours flown. What is less safe is the impact on the customer of high seating capacity forced on the operators, particularly the charter companies, by the accountants. Another factor that might be relevant is attempted cost savings on aircraft maintenance. There has been concern among air transport experts in recent years about the quality of engineers and mechanics. On paper, at least, the procedures for aircraft maintenance are thorough and engineers say that they are as fool-proof as you can get. Key parts have to be replaced after a certain number of flights. Aircraft manufacturers say that the age of the airline does not matter as much as its flying hours. Most airlines choose to replace the parts before the official deadlines. So most aircraft that are 20 years old have been overhauled completely on several occasions; many have been stripped down and almost completely rebuilt. All maintenance work has to be supervised by a qualified engineer and work on the most important parts, such as control surfaces, should be checked by another engineer.

Traditionally, pilot error is also often blamed for serious aviation accidents, such as crashes. After the Coventry crash of a Boeing 737-200 freighter in 1994, it emerged that the Algerian crew had exceeded the length of duty that British pilots are allowed to fly and was making its fifth flight during a night shift that ostensibly was due to last at least ten hours. The report by the Air Accident Investigation branch showed that the crew did not carry out a number of basic procedures and made many mistakes.

More recently, attention has somewhat shifted to inadequate airline management. William Gaillard, a senior official of the IATA, proposed that airlines should submit themselves voluntarily to safety audits to increase public confidence in their performance. Although 75 per cent of accidents were caused by human error, this was not necessarily by pilots but by managements, by reducing spending on maintenance, for example. Line management responsibility for health and safety is a key factor. In JAL a team of maintenance engineers is assigned to each of its aircraft with the team leader's name displayed in the cockpit. When a pilots encounter a problem, they can refer to the team leader who has a close knowledge of that aircraft and would be able to deal with the fault at once. Such thinking is very much in keeping with the principles of Total Quality Management but its feasibility must be affected by sub-contracting of maintenance work.

One of the biggest cargo airlines in the world has one of the worst safety records in the industry and these have been attributed to severe management problems. Critics have argued that this company can be 'amateurish', partly because senior managers have achieved promotion through 'who they know, rather than what they know'. The airline has been accused of fast-tracking ex-military personnel, rather than those trained by civilians and many of its pilots learn to fly in the air force which some experts argue is the wrong kind of training. This has led to internal conflict and poor morale. An internal company report alleged that an authoritarian culture in the cockpit, inadequate English and pilot error were combining to compromise safety.

By contrast, Reason (1993) asked 'should we not be studying what makes organizations relatively safe, rather than focusing on their moments of unsafety? Would it not be a good idea to identify the safest carrier, the most reliable maintainer and the best Air Traffic Control System and then try to find out what makes them good and whether or not their ingredients could be bottled and handed on?' In a spirited response to this challenge, Braithwaite and colleagues (1998:61) tried to focus on what an apparently safe system – that of Australia – did correctly.

> Advances in the area of human factors or organizational safety require more than leadership by bad example which has tended to be the focus of a lot of training in this area. For personnel being trained in the areas of crew resource management (CRM), the emphasis has tended to be on videos or case studies of where things went wrong: E.g. Air Ontario F-28, Dryden; British Midland B737, Kegworth; United Airlines DC-8, Portland. It is only recently that airlines have started to use examples of where people have performed well or used good CRM.

This research into the factors underlying Australia's good air safety record again drew attention to the importance of cultural factors that may exist at several levels from work group or organizational level to industry or even national level. Even with the continued movement to multiculturalism, organizational and national culture will continue to influence behaviour. As Hayward (1997) facetiously observed, 'while a solution to creating a culture-free environment has been proposed – fill it with Australians – in practice, even this does not work'.

Reference to culture in relation to health and safety signifies the need for a managed approach to this aspect of motivation – an overall climate of safety awareness. However, this must be in addition to technical controls that act upon the working environment and its physical characteristics. 'Recent international research seems to indicate that cabin crew are exposed to a range of health and safety risks about which they receive little – if any – information. Exposure to poor air quality in cabins, to ozone, and, to the risk of contracting infectious diseases, represents serious short and long term health and safety risks to flight attendants.' (Boyd & Bain, 1998:17). Like it or not, continuing competitive pressures to lower costs, whilst good for the consumer in some ways, in threatening the welfare of producers of the service, also threaten that of consumers. 'Despite the availability of technologies that could provide fresh air in the cabin to a standard similar to that provided to pilots in the flight deck, the airlines have chosen not to adopt such measures.' (Boyd & Bain,1998:26).

Not that the hardware provided for pilots is as up-to-date as it might be. In a letter to *The Independent* (29 February, 2000), Steve Last who was due to retire after more than 34 years as BA's most senior 747-400 pilot, reflected on the antiquity of airline production hardware alongside the marketing of e-commerce:

> Airlines willingly apply modern techniques to getting the customer to part with his money but the information tools provided to operational personnel – such as flight and cabin crews and engineers – for resolving practical problems on the front line have scarcely improved since the 1960s. As a pilot in February 2000 – an era of instant global access to critical information – I was still working from loose-leaf manuals, cross-referencing and interpolating multiple tables by eye, doing calculations by mental arithmetic and maintaining the condition of a £100 million 'seat-mile factory' with the carbon copy of hand-written notes, just as my predecessors did in 1950. In 20 years time those curious to see what the information 'Stone Age' was like will have to look no further than the flight deck of an airliner.

As a final comment on human resource management in airlines, this encapsulates the potential employee relations conflicts between business and organization, change management and capital equipment, in the same sense that business process re-engineering and other management techniques can be used only in the light of human relationships and existing organizational realities. Despite the rather grandiose strategic alliances among the major carriers, the airline industry remains a sector where local production and operations management and co-operation with employees is a vital element in customer satisfaction. Employees are more than factors of production and will resist authoritarian management, using various devices to recover autonomy. Successful human resource management often requires recognition of the validity of such tactics and successful negotiation with the work groups.

Bibliography

Aldridge, A. (1986) *Power, Authority and Restrictive Practices: A Theoretical Essay in Industrial Relations*, Blackwell.

Al-Jazzaf, Mohammed I. (1999) 'The Impact of privatization on airlines' performance: an empirical analysis', *Journal of Air Transport Management*, 5(1).

Anthony, P.D. (1986) *The Foundation of Management*, Tavistock Publications.

Arthur, C. (1998) 'Airline fare wars move to the web', *The Independent*, 21 September.

Barrie, C. (1997) 'Pilots make peace with cash-strapped BA', *The Independent*, 21 January.

Barry, W.S. (1965) *Airline Management*, Allen & Unwin.

Beavis, S. (1994) 'Maker Threatens Chapter 11 Lines', *The Guardian*, 6 September.

Bellos, A. (1991) 'Fly Girls', *The Guardian*, 19 January.

Benbow, N. (1994) 'Raising the standard: a survey of managers' attitudes to customer care', Institute of Management.

Bentley, S. (2000) 'BA Chief faces flak over Ayling pay-off', *Daily Express*, 12 July.

Blois, K.J. (1992) 'Carlzon's *Moments of Truth* – A critical appraisal', *International Journal of Service Industry Management*, 3(3): 5-18.

Borisov, V., Fairbrother, P. and Clarke, S. (1994) 'Is there room for an independent trade unionism in Russia?' *British Journal of Industrial Relations*.

Boulard, J.C. and Bonnais, R. (1975) Chapter 7 of J.P. Page, ed., *Profil Economique de la France*, Documentation Française, Paris.

Boyd, C. and Bain, P. (1998) 'Once I get you up there, where the air is rarified: health, safety and the working conditions of airline cabin crews', *New Technology, Work and Employment*, 13(1).

Braithwaite, C.R., Caves, R.E. and Faulkner, J.P.E. (1998) 'Australian aviation safety – observations from the lucky country', *Journal of Air Transport Management*, 4(1).

Brown, R. (2000) 'Reach for the sky', *The Independent*, 19 January.

Brown, W. (1983) 'Britain's Unions: New pressures and shifting loyalties', *Personnel Management*, October: 48-51.

Brummer, A. (1995) 'Airlines climb out of doldrums', *The Guardian*, 25 April.

Bryman, A. (1996) 'Leadership in Organizations', in S.R. Clegg, C. Hardy and W. Nord (eds.), *Handbook of Organization Studies*. Sage.

Buckingham, L. (1997) 'Investors threaten to bring Mr. Ayling back to earth', *The Guardian*, 20 July.

Calder, S. (2000) 'Passengers face new departures', *The Independent*, 28 March.

Capelli, P. (1985) 'Competitive Pressures and Labor Relations in the Airline Industry', *Industrial Relations*, 24(3): 316-338.

Capelli, P. (1987) 'Airlines', in D.B. Lipsky and C.B. Donn (eds.) *Collective Bargaining in American Industry*, D.C. Heath, pp.135-186.

Carlzon, J. (1987) *Moments of Truth*, Ballinger Publishing Co.

Chandler, A. (1962) *Strategy and Structure: Chapters in the History of the Industrial Enterprise*, MIT Press.

Chandler, A. (1977) *The Visible Hand: The Managerial Revolution in American Business*, Harvard University Press.

Chandler, M.K. (1964) *Management Rights and Union Interests*. McGraw-Hill.

Chen, C.C. and Meindl, J.R. (1991) 'The construction of leadership images in the popular press: the case of Donald Burr and People Express', *Administrative Science Quarterly*, 36: 521-551.

Chin, A., Hooper, P. and Oum, T.H. (1999) 'The Impact of Asian Economic Crisis on Asian Airlines: short run responses and long run effects', *Journal of Air Transport Management*, 5(2).

Chow, L. (1997) 'Australia's Qantas cuts costs, rather than expanding routes', *Far Eastern Economic Review*, 1 July.

Clark, J. (1993) 'Procedures and consistency versus flexibility and commitment in employee relations', *Human Resource Management Journal*, 4(1).

Clement, B. (1999) 'BA faces inter-union row as cabin crew join AEEU', *The Independent*, 14 March.

Cope, N. (2000) 'BA joins forces to form cost-cutting e-hub', *The Independent*, 28 April.

Cowe, R. (1992) 'The GPA Flotation', *The Guardian*, 12 June.

Dahrendorf, R. (1959) *Class and class conflict in Industrial Society*, Routledge and Kegan Paul.

Deming, W.E. (1988) *Out of the Crisis: Quality, Productivity and Competitive Position*, Cambridge University Press.

Doganis, R. (1991) *Flying Off Course: The Economics of International Airlines*, Harper Collins.

Done, K. and Odell, M. (2000) 'BA seeks to protect its routes over Atlantic', *Financial Times*, 27 January.

Eaton, J. (1993)'Air France's Strategic Plan: Benevolent New Despotism?' *Work, Employment and Society*, 7(4): 585-602.

Eaton, J. (1994) 'The Crazy Economics of Air Freight', *Intereconomics*, 23(1).

Fuller, L. and Smith, V. (1991) 'Consumers' Reports: management by customers in a changing economy', *Work, Employment and Society*, 5(1): 1-16.

Gardner, D. (2000) 'India's renewed privatization thrust fails to dispel a sense of déjà vu'.

Gil, A. (1990) 'Air Transport Deregulation and its Implications for Flight Attendants', *International Labour Review*, 29(3).

Goleman, D. (2000) 'Leadership that gets results', *Harvard Business Review*, March-April.

Gonzalez, J. (2000) 'Interview with Stephan Egli' *El Mundo*, 9 July.

Green, D. (1992) 'Air Freight takes fright at the gravity of recession', *Financial Times*, 19 August.

Gustafsson, A., Ekdahl, F. and Edvardsson, B. (1999) 'Customer-focussed service development in practice – a case study at Scandinavian Airlines System', *International Journal of Service Industry Management*, 10(4).

Hanlon, P. (1996) *Global Airlines*, Butterworth Heinemann.

Harper, K (1990) 'Pilots get 1992-style trade union negotiations off to a flying start', *The Guardian*, 10 August.

Harper, K (1996) 'Fly me, I work for half pay. Smiles are obligatory', *The Guardian*, 14 December.

Harper, K. (1996) 'BA to shed 5,000 jobs to hone competitive edge', *The Guardian*, 24 July.

Harper, K. (1997) 'BA faces strike in dispute over catering sell-off', *The Guardian* 3 June.

Harper, K. (1997) 'BA in threat to sue staff after vote backs strike', *The Guardian*, 26 June.

Harper, K. (1999) 'Rivals besiege airline that fell from grace', *The Guardian*, 9 November.

Harris, S. (1995) 'The Business of Leadership', *Business Life*, December.

Harrison, M. (2000) 'Airbus signs up Emirates and Air France in superjumbo war', *The Independent*, 25 July.

Harrison, M. (1998) 'Bad conditions may ground BA's US deal', *The Independent*, 13 October.

Harrison, M. (1999) 'Heathrow, we have a problem: Can Bob Ayling put the wheels back on BA?' *The Independent*, 26 May.

Harrison, M. (1999) 'BA protests at Midland deal', *The Independent*, 21 October.

Harrison, M. (1999) 'BA suffers defeat over plan to merge pension fund schemes', *The Independent*, 17 November.

Harrison, M. (1999) 'Iberia on runway to flotation as BA takes £160m. stake', *The Independent*, 16 December.

Harrison, M. (1999) 'Branson raises £600m. from Virgin airline sale to fund net expansion', *The Independent*, 21 December.

Harrison, M. (2000) 'Ayling warns of catastrophe for world's airlines', *The Independent*, 19 May.

Harrison, M. (2000) 'Virgin warns against sell-out in air talks', *The Independent*, 12 June.

Harrison, M. (2000) 'BA merger with KLM would lead to loss of 16,200 jobs', *The Independent*, 22 June.

Harrison, M. and Usborne, D. (2000) 'US alliance opens door to shake-up in air industry', *The Independent*, 25 May.

Hayward, B. (1997) 'Culture, Crew Resource Management and Aviation Safety', Paper presented to 1976 Australian and New Zealand Societies of Air Safety Inspectors seminar, *Aviation Safety for the 21st Century in the Asia-Pacific Region*, Brisbane.

Henderson, H. (1993) *Paradigms in Progress*, Adamantine Press.

Hinthorne, T. (1996) 'Predatory Capitalism, Pragmatism and Legal Positivism in the Airlines Industry', *Strategic Management Journal, 17.*

Hirsch, F. (1997) *Social Limits to Growth*, Routledge and Kegan.

Hochschild, A. (1983) *The Managed Heart*, University of California Press.

Hope, K. (1999) 'Speedwing sees profitability as Olympic Ideal', *Financial Times*, 27 July.

Hopfle, H. (1993) 'Culture and Commitment: British Airways' in D. Gowler, K. Legge and C. Clegg (eds.), *Case Studies in Organizational Behaviour and Human Resource Management*, Paul Chapman.

International Labour Organisation, (1990) *Report: Structural Change in civil aviation. Implications for personnel management.* Geneva, International Labour Office.

Ioannides, D. and Debbage, K. (1997) 'Post-Fordism and Flexibility: the Travel Industry Polyglot', *Tourism Management*, 18(4).

Jackson, T. (1995) *Virgin King*, Harper Collins.

Jayasankaran, S. (1999) 'Gaining Speed', *Far Eastern Economic Review*, 1 July.

Karp, J. (1997) 'Open and Shut Skies', *Far Eastern Economic Review*, 6 February.

Kay, J. (1991) 'Identifying the Strategic Market', *Business Strategy Review*, 1(1).

KPMG/International Air Transport Association, (1992) *Survey of accounting policies, disclosure and financial trends in the inter-national airline industry.*

Landers, P. (1998) 'Flying into Trouble', *Far Eastern Economic Review*, 25 July.

Luce, E. (1996) 'Philippine Airlines ready for new take-off', *Financial Times*, 5 July.

Mabey, C., Salaman, G. and Storey, J. (1998) *Human Resource Management: A Strategic Introduction*, Blackwell.

Mackie, L. (1987) 'Slavery at 20,000 feet', *The Guardian,* 17 June.

Mallet, V. (1992) 'Uneasy peace reigns at Thailand's national airline', *Financial Times*, 7 September.

Mars, G. (1982) *Cheats at Work*, Allen and Unwin.

Marsh, P. (2000) 'BA to unveil new travel agent payment structure', *Financial Times*, 24 January.

Marshall, A. (2000) 'Virgin to lose Chicago slot as transatlantic open skies row intensifies', *The Independent,* 29 March.

McCabe, D. (1999) 'Total Quality Management: Anti-Union Trojan Horse or Management Albatross?' *Work, Employment and Society*, 13(4).

Milne, S. (1997a) 'Lost pay, lost time, lost expectation, lost trust', *The Guardian,* 11 July.

Milne, S. (1997b) 'Foreign unions pledge to support BA strikers', *The Guardian,* 14 July.

Milner, M. (1996) 'Air France president's plan flies in face of pilots' strike', *The Guardian,* 8 July.

Mintzberg, H. (1987) 'Crafting Strategy', *Harvard Business Review*, July/August.

Murphy, D. (1999) 'Weighed Down', *Far Eastern Economic review*, 14 October.

Northrup, H.R. (1985) 'The New Industrial Relations Climate in the Airlines', *Industrial and Labor Relations Review,* 36(2): 167-181.

Oakland, J. (1993) *Total Quality Management*, Butterworth-Heinemann.

Odagiri, H. (1984) 'The Firm as a collection of human resources' in P. Wiles and G. Routh (eds.) *Economics in Disarray*. Blackwell.

Ohanessian, E. and Kleiner, B.H. (1999) 'Managing Human Behaviour in the Airline industry', *Management Research News*, 22(2).

Oliver, N. and Wilkinson, R. (1989) 'Strategic Fit: the real lesson from Japan', *University of Wales Review of Economics & Business*, 4:3-8.

Oum, T.H. and Yu, C. (1998) 'An analysis of profitability of the world's major airlines', *Journal of Air Transport Management*, 4(4).

Overbeek, H. (1990) *Global Capitalism and National Decline*. Unwin Hyman.

Pain, D. (1997) 'Punters bale out of BA as union power play backfires', *The Independent*, 22 July.

Pascale, R. (1990) *Managing on the Edge*, Penguin Business Management.

Payton, S. (1998) 'Web holder the key to cut-price travelling', *The Independent*, 17 November.

Pedersini, R. (1999) "Virtual Strike" held at Meridiana Airline. European Foundation for Living and Working Conditions.

Piganiol, C. (1989) 'Industrial Relations and Enterprise Restructuring in France', *International Labour Review*, 128, 5, 623-634.

Pinchemel, P. (1987) *France: A Survey*, Cambridge University Press.

Price, A. (1997) *Human Resource Management in a Business Context*, International Thomson Business Press.

Prokesch, S.E. (1995) 'Competing on Service: Interview with Sir Colin Marshall', Harvard Business Review.

Ramesh, R. (1998) 'Air France's £2bn aid is ruled illegal', *The Independent*, 26 June.

Reason, J. (1993) 'Human Factors in Aviation', Proceedings of the 22nd IATA Technical Conference, Montreal.

Reed, A. (1985) 'Air Freight; Special Report', *The Times*, 20 September.

Rhoades, D.L. and Waguespack, B. (1999) 'Better safe than service? The relationship between service and safety quality in the US airline industry', *Managing Service Quality*, 9(6).

Riley, B.K. (1999) 'Using non-financial information to predict financial performance: the case of the US airline industry', *Journal of Accounting, Auditing and Finance*, 14(1).

Root, K. (1999) 'Should you Invest in Air Travel?' *the Independent*, 9 June.

Saeed Shah, (2000) 'British Airways to stop paying commission to travel agents', *The Independent*, 24 January.

Sayles, L.R. (1958) *The Behaviour of Industrial Work Groups*, Wiley.

Seal, J. and Kleiner, B.H. (1999) 'Managing Behaviour in the Airline Industry', *Management Research News*, 2/3.

Seritsö, H. (1996) 'The Executive view on the cost problem of European airlines', *European Business Review*, 4.

Seritsö, H. and Vepsalainen, A.P. (1997) 'Airline Cost Drivers: Cost implications of fleet, routes and personnel policies', *Journal of Air Transport Management*, 3(1).

Sheehan, B. and Geary, J. (1999) 'TEAM Aer Lingus employees seek deal prior to potential sell-off', Gir.online.European Foundation for Improvement of Living and Working Conditions.

Simonian, H. (1992) Interview with Giovanni Basignani, *Financial Times*, 7 September.

Skinner, W.H. (1981) 'Bag Hat, No Cattle: Managing Human Resources', *Harvard Business Review*, September-October: 106.

Smith, V. (1990) *Managing in the Corporate Interest*, University of California Press.

Smithers, R (1995) 'Deaths in Air Accidents Increase by 25 per cent', *The Guardian*, 17 January.

Spinks, P. (1994) 'Dutch airline flies in face of recession', *The Guardian*, 3 December.

Springett, P. (1997) 'BA refuses to be drawn on £135m. China Airlines stake', *The Guardian*, 1 January.

Stogdill, R.M. (1950) 'Leadership, membership and organization', *Psychological Bulletin*, 47.

Taylor, P. (1992) 'The Aim of a Global Ring', *Financial Times*, 25 September.

Taylor, S. and Tyler, M. (2000) 'Emotional Labour and Sexual Difference in the Airline Industry', *Work, Employment and Society*, 14(1).

Thorpe, V. (1998) 'BA in-flight meal was a dog's dinner says Ronay', *The Indpendent*, 26 October.

Tieman, R. (2000) 'Controls set for open skies', *Financial Times*, 26 January.

Tory, P. (2000) 'Pilot test hits turbulence', *Sunday Express*, 16 April.

Tyler, M. and Abbott, P. (1998) 'Chocs Away: Weight Watching in the Contemporary Airline Industry', *Sociology*, 32(3).

Usborne, D. (1998) 'American pilots retire early to avoid stock market crash', *The Independent*, 9 October.

Usborne, D. (1999) 'US lauches crackdown on shoddy airlines', *The Independent*, 11 March.

Verkaik, R. (1999) 'Mother's victory on long hours',*The Independent*, 7 August.

Walsh, D.J. (1994) *On Different Planes: An Organizational Analysis of Co-operation Among Airline Unions*, ILR Press.

Walters, J. (1994) 'With One Bound Lufthansa is Free', *The Observer*, 11 September.

Walters, J. (1997) 'Looking for Industrial Action', *The Observer*, 6 July.

Walton, R.E. (1985) 'From Control to Commitment in the workplace', *Harvard Business Review*, March-April.

Warhurst, R. (1996) 'Converging on HRM? Change and Continuity in European Airlines Industrial Relations', *European Journal of Industrial Relations*, 1(2).

Weick, K.E. and Westley, F. (1996) 'Organizational Learning: Affirming an Oxymoron', in S.R. Clegg, C. Hardy and W. Nord (eds.) *Handbook of Organization Studies*, Sage.

Weiser, C.R. (1995) 'Championing the Customer', *Harvard Business Review*, November-December.

Wentworth, K. (1995) ISA Survey on Sexual Harassment and Gender Discrimination, ISA.

Westlake, M. (1991) 'Spreading their Wings', *Far Eastern Economic Review*, 151(5): 35-37.

Westlake, M. (1993) 'In battered shape: strike bruises Cathay Pacific', *Far Eastern Economic Review*, 25, March.

Westlake, M. and Jayasankaran. (1999) 'A Tale of Two Airlines', *Far Eastern Economic Review*, 1 July.

Wheatcroft, S. (1964) *Air Transport Policy*. Michael Joseph.

White, O.F. and Wolf, J.F. (1995) 'Deming's Total Quality Management Movement and the Baskin Robbins Problem, Part 1: Is it Time to go back to Vanilla?' *Administration and Society*, 2(2).

Williams, D. (1988) 'Banking and Changes in Industry Structure', in T. Barker and P. Dunne (eds.) *The British Economy after Oil: Manufacturing or services?* Croom-Helm.

Williamson, O.E. (1975) *Markets and Hierarchies*, Free Press, Macmillan.

Windle, R.J. (1991) 'The world's airlines: A cost and productivity comparison', *Journal of Transport Economics and Policy*, 25, January: 31-49.

Woodcock, A. (2000) 'Airline caterer offers jobs to sacked staff', *The Independent*, 24 April.

Wouters, J. (1989) The Sociology of Emotions and Flight Attendants: Hochschild's '*Managed Heart*', *Theory Culture and Society*, 6.

Zuckerman, L. (1999) 'Mistrust at Full Throttle', *International Tribune*, 16 February.

Index